MW00715061

LIES
MY KID'S TEACHER
TOLD ME!

How parents can better understand
the school system, and help
their children be successful in it.

JOY SMITH

EDUCATIONAL ENTERPRISES
Winnipeg, Manitoba, Canada

*To my children, and all
the parents of children
I write for.*

C. Educational Enterprises
All Rights Reserved
1994

ISBN 1-55056-315-7
Printed in Canada

TABLE OF CONTENTS

ACKNOWLEDGMENTS

This book was inspired by the many parents I've met and talked to about education and educational standards. I was overwhelmed by their passionate concern for higher educational standards for their children.

Others moved me by their heart felt dilemma over what to do when their children were having problems in this gigantic machine known as the educational system.

The soul of this book is comprised of all the excellent teaching practices I've seen in the system which were hidden by mediocrity. Master teachers have moved me to write about 'how to recognize excellent teaching practices'. I hope this book will renew their energy and let them know their work is not unrecognized, and that they do make a difference!

I want to thank Kate Thomas of "Here's How Marketing" who gave me the idea for the title. Her enthusiasm is infectious!

I want to thank my lovely daughter, Janet, who spent many hours attending seminars with me, and in the organization of this book. Her faith in my work has been an inspiration to me!

This book was driven by my partner, my confidante and critic, my husband. His high teaching standard and genuine care about the education of children have been a source of energy to me. He told me to "dream a dream, believe in it, have faith in it and show love for it....and your dream will come true".

I have done all that. Perhaps in some small way, this book will help some parent or some child, sometime.

PREFACE

Today's educational system is a complicated place to be.

There is a public outcry for higher standards and more discipline. Parents are in shock over the lack of the right to hold a child back a grade when the child has not obtained an acceptable standard, particularly when ability levels enables him/her to do so. Teachers are caught in the middle of parental pressure and the educational system's monstrous machine, zapping out new curriculum, more expectations and less respect and authority in the classroom setting.

Children today are in the minority when they live in a two parent family situation - particularly if those people are their biological parents. They face insurmountable pressure from peers. Economic constraints and unemployment have impacted on families in a big way.

All of these factors reflect what happens in the classroom. When students reach the higher grades, often they are surprised to find themselves not making the grade. Others peer into the future and wonder what the job market will hold for them when they do graduate.

Educators are faced with rapidly changing technology and antiquated curricula. The lack of leadership at the administrative level has left teachers with a variety of "band wagons" to join, and little else.

Master teachers go unrecognized and either fade into the woodwork, remain undercover in their classrooms, or give up.

What to do? Get involved! Teachers need to speak up and dare to raise the standard of academic achievement - the very thing they were originally hired to do! They need to become more accountable to parents for the pedagogical practices they use when they teach. Dynamic administrators need to take a leadership role in the educational system. Less attention to the political concerns and more time spent on curriculum management and child development would do much to improve matters in the school setting. Administrators need to become more accountable to the public for the programs put in place and the monies spent in education.

Parents need to take responsibility for disruptive children. They need to become good role models for their children and provide stability for them in this busy world.

It is a well known fact that there is a direct correlation between children who come from homes that value education and success in school, and those who don't.

In contrast, when a positive attitude toward learning and academic achievement is not fostered in the home, lack of caring and irresponsible behaviors in school are evident.

The school is not a drop off site for the nation's children. It only works if there is a partnership coupled with trust and mutual respect between home and school.

This trust and mutual respect will flourish if teachers open the doors and allow parents in. The more parents understand about the school system, the more they will be empowered to support their children's learning in a meaningful way.

All things considered, it is mandatory that parents and educators strive toward a common goal - the education of our children within the context of higher standards and excellence.

Educators have to stop saying "everything is wonderful" every time a question is asked. Parents need to work in partnership with the school to enhance their children's educational progress. To do this they have to become more knowledgeable about how the system works and how to recognize good and bad teaching practices. They need to learn to ask the right questions and expect the right answers.

This book attempts to open a window through which parents can see and a door through which they can enter.

CHAPTER 1

Introduction

This is a "handbook" written for parents. Today's schools can be a scary place for parents. I know of a woman who, upon entering a school building, lost her courage, turned around and walked out again. Not five minutes after having entered the school grounds, she had the experience of hearing her car license number aired over the school P.A. system, coupled with a request for her to move the car because she parked in a reserved parking spot! On her way out the door she tripped over some building blocks left unthinkingly in a precarious spot in the hallway. Hardly a welcoming experience for anyone ! Too often parents experience less than happy episodes when they are placed in a school setting.

On another occasion, a parent was reluctant to go into the school because she had the perception that the teachers were "talking down" to her when she attempted to express concern over her child's progress. The gap between the teacher, the Principal and the parent needs to be cemented into a partnership which is centered on the well being of the child.

Our schools would strengthen if we tapped our most valuable resource - *our parents.*

There are ways of working with the school your child attends. It does not have to be threatening or scary. This handbook describes the settings, decodes some of the jargon and provides strategies for parents to use when problems arise.

Parents ask many questions like...

1. How do I know if the school in my district will provide the type of education and emotional support my child needs?

2. How can my child obtain a strong academic standing?

3. How do I approach the teacher when I want to volunteer in my child's classroom?

4. How do I deal with anxieties my child has about school?

5. What do I do when my child doesn't like the teacher?

6. What do I do when I'm not satisfied with the education my child is receiving in his/her classroom?

7. My child's report card doesn't tell me anything. How can I persuade the teacher to tell me exactly where my child stands academically?

8. My school is bringing in new programs I have never heard about. How do I know these new programs are good for my child?

9. Why doesn't the school system teach the basics anymore?

10. I want my child to be tested so I know exactly where he is academically in Math, Reading, and Writing. How do I have the proper testing done on my child?

The listed questions are all ones parents have asked me at seminars I have given. Since these are questions parents have; then they need to be answered.

There are many concerned parents who do not feel a part of their children's school experience. They are afraid their children will not be prepared to face the academic challenges at the post secondary level.

This is not an attempt by parents to undermine the present day educational system. Rather, it is a demand to be a part of their children's education. It is a reflection of the concern parents have to insure their children receive a higher standard within the context of the educational system, and go out into the world well prepared.

CHAPTER 2

Questions Commonly Asked By Parents

This book was written to take the mystery out of educational jargon and to enable the layman to understand the present day school system.

There are many ways of working with the school your children attend. It doesn't have to be a threatening or intimidating experience! The following provides strategies for parents to use when problems arise.

Here are some queries posed by concerned parents:

Question:
How do I know if the school in my neighborhood will provide the type of education and emotional support my child needs?
Answer:
Shop around! Visit your neighborhood schools. Make appointments to meet the Principal. Visit the school - get the feel of it! Ask questions. Prepare a set of questions before you visit the school. That way you will not miss out any important points you want to talk about.

Try to get to know parents who already send their children to the school. Ask them questions. Every school has it's strengths and weaknesses. Make it your business to find out what these are - your child depends on you doing your homework!

Question:
My child is having a great deal of difficulty in Math. He has never understood it. What can I do? I feel he has asked for more help but still doesn't understand it.
Answer:
Often difficulty in Math stems from missing pieces of the puzzle. Math is like playing the piano, it takes constant practice and hard work. When a student has missed a concept that later restricts him/her

from learning, it is because he/she doesn't have the building blocks.

A student like this should be tested to see if he/she is weak in some area. Then he/she should review basic concepts and work through problems related to that concept. Consistent study habits are essential in Math. It is a precise subject in that each skill has to be built upon. Sometimes it is necessary to meet with the teacher to schedule after school instruction to enhance the students' level of mastery.

Here's an interesting point to ponder. Many teachers, who volunteer their own time for before or after school math classes, find that attendance is low.

Question:
I've tried to have my son held back for the past two years. I've been told that there is a "no fail policy" and it would harm his self image and self esteem. I feel strongly that it would do him good to be held back a grade. What can I do?
Answer:
A "'no fail policy" in a school division means that no child should be "failed" a grade or in other words, be required to remain in the same grade for another year.

If a parent feels strongly that his/her child would benefit from remaining in the grade another year, they should go through the chain of command. Firstly, discuss it with the teachers and the Principal. If there are no results, a parent can see the Superintendent and attempt to get results there. Ultimately, the School Board can be contacted to air your concerns. Follow your convictions. A parent has every right to push for what he/she feels is best for his/her child!

Question:
How do I know if my child is achieving the academic skills he/she needs to maintain a strong academic standing?
Answer:
Each province or state is required to follow a provincial or state curriculum guidelines. Copies of these guidelines can be obtained from the Provincial or State Departments of Education. Copies of curriculum guides can be found in every school as well.

These curriculum guides are available in every academic discipline...Math, Science, Language Arts, Social Studies, etc. They outline what is to be taught at every grade level. Parents can obtain these curriculum guides and compare what units of study their child is experiencing at school.

Being aware of what your child is learning enables the parent to support what is happening at school. If the parent feels his/her child is not obtaining adequate academic instruction, he/she can question what is happening. Interaction with the classroom teacher is important to enable parents to understand what is happening with their child.

Question:
Should my child go to a private school next year?
Answer:
This would depend on what goals and objectives the parent has for the child. Generally, parents opt for this direction if they feel the child is not acquiring strong basic academic skills in the public system. Sometimes parents want their child to be in an 'all girls' or 'all boys' school to try and diminish boy/girl distractions. Parents will seek out schools that offer challenging programs for high academic students. They send their children to private schools with reputations for academic excellence.

Question:
Should my child be put in a room with her best friend next year?
Answer:
Often students are more secure and comfortable when they have a good friend in class. If the best friend is a negative influence, it is better to separate the students. Students need all the positive reinforcement they can get. If a best friend is continually bombarding your son or daughter with 'school sucks', then it might be time for a change. Generally speaking, however, good friends are best left together.

Question:
Should I hire a tutor to help my child?
Answer:
If finances are not a concern, and the child is weak in an academic subject, hiring a competent tutor could be beneficial. Many high schools keep lists of above average students who are willing to tutor for extra spending money. Catching the problem early is good advice. Don't wait until grade 11 to hire a tutor. If it's affordable, get a jump on

the problem in the elementary years.

Although teachers are not required to give lessons before or after school, many teachers do so. Consult your local school to find out what is available for your child.

Question:
Why do teachers tell me not to worry about my child's spelling. They tell me it will remedy itself in time. Is this true?
Answer:
This belief is part of the whole language approach. Most students need some formal spelling in combination with whole language. It is the rare student who self evaluates and improves his own spelling.

Whole language has strong points - but spelling should be taught in combination with phonics, and formal spelling practices.

Spelling doesn't remedy itself - it takes practice!

Question:
Why isn't school challenging?
Answer:
If schools aren't challenging, it's because, as a rule, they teach to the middle and lower thinking skills. Bright and average children are often left out because they do not spend 50% of their time in the upper level thinking skills and in problem solving. Too much of the teacher's time and efforts are spent on the average to below average learner. The parent needs to meet with the teacher and make sure his/her child is being challenged.

Question:
Does my child have to take French or Music when he / she hates those subjects?
Answer:
The school program set out for School Divisions originates with set Provincial or State guidelines. Even the required number of minutes is set out for the teachers to teach. All children are required to get a general education. Consequently, these children are obligated to take French and Music. Also, it is good for children to learn that they are not going to enjoy everything. It is okay for them to study subjects that are not their favorite. It builds self discipline!

Question:
How is my child relating to his/her peers this year?
Answer:

This is a question commonly asked by parents of very shy students - or parents whose child fights or quarrels with other children. Parents should consider counseling if the child is very troubled constantly about not relating to his/her peers. As we all know, it is very hurtful sometimes to be left out. The ostracized individual is often consumed with thoughts of self doubt.

Question:
Does my son have to work with someone else on a project? Can he work alone?
Answer:

Most teachers would be pleased to allow a student to work on his own, if this would benefit the child. Sometimes teachers like students to work together because they learn from each other. Discuss this concern with the teacher.

Question:
Is it really necessary to have so much homework?
Answer:

There is much to learn at school. There are times when homework is essential to help the student acquire a solid understanding of what is being taught. If a student has an unusually heavy schedule or if a personal dilemma has interfered with the homework routine, the teacher should be contacted. Most teachers would understand that some circumstances can prevent homework from being completed on time. However, if the parent objects to homework, the teacher usually relents and the student 'misses out' or doesn't keep up with the class. Teachers should not pile homework on for the sake of doing homework. It should be an extension of what is being taught in class. Parents need to support this and help teach their children the value of hard work and consistent study habits. This doesn't always happen.

Question:
Could you give my child more homework?
Answer:

This question usually comes from concerned parents who are worried their child is not receiving the basic skills needed to go on to higher education. Teachers should listen to a request such as this.

Question:
Do you assign homework? Why does my daughter tell me she has no homework, when the teacher says there is homework?
Answer:
If the teacher says there is homework, the parent should find out when it is assigned and what the expectations for completion are. Homework books are good sources of information for parents. These books are sent home everyday and parents are requested to sign them so they know what is requested of their child. Usually, if the daughter says she has no homework, and the teacher says she does, she's either 'playing games' with her parents, or does not understand what is expected of her. It is also possible that the teacher assigned homework and the student completed it during class time.

Question:
My child hates school! Why does he feel this way?
Answer:
Find out if there is a personality conflict between teacher and child, or if the student is having problems with his peers. Sometimes when a child says he hates school it is because he fears school for some reason.
Lack of success in anything academic may be at the heart of the problem. Parents need to address this as soon as possible. A mole hill in grade one, may be a mountain in grade six. Positive reinforcement will help. Learning must be valued in the home!

Question:
Should my son go to after school basketball or after school math?
Answer:
You should decide what your priorities are as a family - academics or sports. There are times when a child needs some physical activity to release tensions. However, children also have to learn that responsible behavior toward their academics will pay off later.

Question:
My daughter refuses to read at home. What can I do?
Answer:

From my experience those who 'hate' reading really cannot read. Frustration at continually having to do something she can't do is at the root of the hatred. Find out what interests your daughter. Subscribe to magazines. Buy comics for her to read! Hook her into reading on a regular basis. After she starts reading, introduce her to a variety of novels, books, etc. Non-readers have a great deal of difficulty decoding words and sentences and therefore derive no satisfaction from the experience of reading. You might have to sit with the child and guide her through many books, maybe keeping a record of difficult words. Assist her in the comprehension so at least 'some' enjoyment is derived from the content.

Reading aloud is a powerful technique, also! When a student reads aloud, it eliminates the temptation to cheat or skip words or not read at all. Start with anything your daughter might be interested in...an article from the newspaper, or a recipe! Give her a quiet, relaxing place to read. Turning off the television is beneficial!

Question:
My son hates the music teacher. What can I do?
Answer:

Students are required to obtain a general education K-12. Music is a part of the curriculum. Children are not always going to like every subject equally. They need to develop responsibility toward their studies. However, some teachers need to use better interpersonal skills when working with students. Talk to the music teacher. Get her to interact in a positive way with your child. Music teachers usually see many students from many different classes. Sometimes it is hard for a teacher to understand how a child is feeling when she doesn't see him for extended lengths of time. Be sure and make her aware of how your son is feeling!

Question:
My son is going into Junior High School. The designated school is unsuitable. We want him enrolled in another one farther away - outside our boundary. How do I get this to happen?
Answer:

Go to your superintendent. Find out what the Division policy is,

9

covering school boundaries. Give your reasons on why you want your child in another school. Often persistence brings results! Most Superintendents are interested in insuring the School Division provides an education suitable to all students. They like to hear from parents, as a rule. That is one of the reasons they were hired.

Question:

My daughter is bothered by the four or five kids who disrupt the lessons all day long. The teacher has invited me to come in and sit in the classroom as an observer. Should I go?
Answer:

If the teacher has invited you to sit and observe, the teacher wants a witness to the disruptive behavior. This would indicate that the teacher needs parental support to have the disruptive student removed for the benefit of all the others.

Question:

I've witnessed disruptive students interrupting my child's learning in class. What can I do now?
Answer:

Go to the Principal and explain your concerns. Explain your child has a right to learn and this disruptive behavior is preventing that from happening. If the Principal is not amenable to helping with this problem, the Superintendent can be contacted. There are several ways of resolving this problem - even changing schools is a possibility!

Question:

We're going on a two week vacation to Florida. Can I take my child out of class?
Answer:

Yes. Most children benefit from vacations. If you are concerned about homework, go to the teacher and prearrange to have some homework to take with you.

Question:

Why don't schools teach grammar anymore?
Answer:

If your school doesn't teach grammar, ask about it. Let them

know your concerns. Parents have a right to make sure their children acquire the basic skills. Grammar skills should be taught. The four basic sentence patterns, including complex sentences, are especially necessary.

Question:
Why, when I read my son's report card, is he evaluating himself? This is done in a friendly letter format.
Answer:
This is a relatively new reporting technique. If you are uncomfortable with it - let them know. Teachers are paid to teach and evaluate students, not to have students recite lesson plans. A student's self evaluation can be part of that - certainly not the whole evaluation! Remember, your son's oral or written report will only be as good as what the teacher has taught.

Question:
Should I sit in a parent / teacher interview and listen to my son evaluate himself? It sounds a little rehearsed.
Answer:
Voice your objections to the teacher. Make sure you receive the evaluation of your child's progress you need to understand the level of mastery he has reached. Consult and compare your child's mastery level to two things - Bloom's Taxonomy and the curriculum. For example, the curriculum might say your son should have mastered the times tables by the end of grade four...has he? He should also be applying these skills in problem solving and in the upper thinking levels.

Question:
Should my child be spending so much time on the computer?
Answer:
Computers are tools to assist learning. However, other basic academic skills are of equal or greater importance. Parents should ask: "Where on a learning continuum do my child's computer activities fall?" Learning how to access software such as Claris Works, or sending messages on the InterNet, may have nothing to do with upper level thinking. Instead, design technology and programming are loftier goals.

Question:
Should my child be learning typing skills in elementary school?
Answer:
Typing skills are usually taught at the high school level. However, some schools teach then earlier because the child spends time on the computer. Typing skills are useful for this purpose. However, the majority of the students school time should not be spent on typing skills. There is precious little time to cover the reading, writing and math skills.

Question:
Should my son opt for the band program?
Answer:
Generally speaking, students in the band program are extending their thinking skills. This is a personal decision your child has to make. However, in my experience as a teacher I have never seen so much 'practicing' occurring as when students reach junior high and receive an instrument. All that practice is great for self discipline.

Question:
My daughter didn't make the team. She's devastated. What can I do?
Answer:
Keep encouraging her! This time will pass. It's part of growing up. Maybe this would be a good time to have some quality time with her. As a result you might both end up in an adult sport such as handball or racquetball. Maybe mom or dad should decide that this is the year you will introduce her to golfing or curling. In the end, parents should be the heroes and role models.

Question:
My child lives just outside the boundary for allowing students into the school lunch program. He needs lunch supervision. How do I get him in the lunch program?
Answer:
Each school is different. Most schools however will 'bend' the rules in cases like this. Don't be shy about asking.

Question:
The school keeps asking that I and my child come in to see the school counselor. I don't want to attend. Do I have to?
Answer:
Try it! Many families have been helped by some counseling. Counselors are usually experts at making people feel comfortable. It doesn't hurt to try.

Question:
What do teachers do on the in-service days? Is it a holiday?
Answer:
No, it is not a holiday! Each in-service has an agenda of meetings centered around school concerns and Division goals. It may be a day off for students - but not for teachers. However, every parent has the right to ask what the teachers will be doing on the in-service days. If a parent has any concerns, he/she should feel free to express their concerns. Quite honestly, there are occasions when in-service days could be put to better use. Principals and teachers need to be vigilant about using in-service days to their best advantage.

Question:
How can my child obtain a strong academic standing?
Answer:
If a student develops consistent study habits and is exposed to appropriate teaching practices, he will obtain an academic standing appropriate to his ability level.

Question:
How do I deal with anxieties my child has about school?
Answer:
Find out what these anxieties are. Talk to the teacher about them. Work as a team to reassure the child, and relieve some of the anxieties.

Question:
What do I do when my child doesn't like the teacher?

Answer:
Sometimes there is a personality clash between teacher and student. This should be discussed with the teacher involved. Work with your child to allow her to develop good interpersonal skills. If the problem does not seem to be resolved, have a meeting with the Principal and the teacher together. Often a third party will diffuse a potentially explosive situation.

Question:
What do I do when I'm not satisfied with the education my child is receiving?
Answer:
First of all, talk with the teacher. Express your concerns. Good teachers are very willing to extend a child's education. A word of caution. Confrontational methods do not usually work. Parents need to be active not only at the classroom level, but also at the School Board level. They need to be vigilant about the programs that are introduced into the school system. Not all ideas or programs work or benefit the students. If you feel your child is not receiving the education you want him to have, them question it! Get to the root of the problem! Ask if the educational standard is poor because of poor educational policies, poor teaching practices, classroom control problems, difficult students, or a combination of things.

Question:
My school is embarking upon a new school wide academic program. I don't know much about it. When I talk to the people at the school they "talk it up" and make it sound wonderful. I have reservations about it for a number of reasons. I just don't know what to do, or think about this. How do I know this is good for my children?
Answer:
Get in contact with schools who already have this program in place. Ask questions about it. Visit the school. Then ask other schools why they _didn't_ put it in place. Talk to teachers from both school settings. Gather what information you can from the Department of Education in your Province or State. By acquiring this information, you will be able to base your judgments on your knowledge and experience, rather than 'gut feelings'. One question to ask, which may act as a quick barometer of the school's sincerity over the new program: "Do you plan

to formally evaluate this program over the next three to five years, to demonstrate a significant improvement in students' academics?"

Question:
    What are the most effective ways parents can be catalysts for change?
Answer:
    Join parent groups. Participate! Be vocal about your concerns, and supportive of good teachers and good teaching practices. Initiate programs by being aware of what is needed in your particular school. If your school is trying to establish a good problem solving program for example, get behind the program. Helping to fund raise for materials needed in classrooms to enable the program to be implemented effectively is of paramount importance. Setting up workshops so you as a parent can become aware of what the problem solving techniques are all about, would be very beneficial for you.
    Extending your child's learning at home by establishing consistent homework habits certainly enhances the academic standing. Fostering responsible attitudes in children towards their studies can not be underestimated. This eliminates half of the problems children will have in school. Parents are an integral part of what makes a school work effectively. Without their influence, and support, schools lack a valuable asset.

CHAPTER 3

Educational Jargon
- and How To Decipher It!

There are many terms used by educators. The following outlines some of these terms and gives simplistic, easy-to-understand definitions.

Whole Language

An approach to teach students how to read, write, communicate and listen. Emphasis is placed on activity based learning. The Whole Language approach downplays the formal teaching of grammar and spelling. Students are encouraged to use their personal, unstructured language, to explore new ideas. In literature studies students are encouraged to interact with literary works.

The Four Strands of Whole Language

These four strands are four components of literacy. They are listening, speaking, reading and writing.

Portfolios

These are simply a type of folder used by the students to "store" their writing. They keep their first, second or third drafts there. Some see it as a program to improve Language Arts skills. How? The students are to save their best samples of writing in the portfolio, and explain why they did so.

Literature Circles

This is where a small group of students will read a novel. They sign a contract to monitor their reading of the novel on daily basis. The students are asked questions about the novel and are encouraged to study the novel in depth. This covers historical background of the novel, character study, plot development, etc.

Bulk Reading

The teachers are instructed to build classroom libraries within the homeroom classroom. Students are encouraged to read a variety of books. Bulk reading is intended to expose students to a wide spectrum of literature in the classroom. It was presumed that the student would then have a heightened interest in reading and literature. A warning: often with bulk reading, there isn't a lot of "bulk comprehension" happening.

ALP
This stands for Alternative Learning Program. If a child is having problems, a special program is designed to meet the child's academic and social needs.

Basal Reader
The basal reader is a collection of structured stories that are accompanied by vocabulary lists, questions centered around the plot and characters in the story. An example of a basal reader is "Mr. Mugs", "Starting Points in Reading", etc.

Editing Groups
Groups of students who evaluate each others writing. They give suggestions for improving their peers' story, grammar and punctuation. They are supposed to take a story written by a peer and improve it.

Group Learning
Here students learn in a child centered, child driven manner. Children evaluating children. Children teaching children.

Mainstreaming
Students who have learning difficulties or behavior problems, or are physically disadvantaged are incorporated into the regular classroom setting. Often if funding permits, an instructional assistant accompanies the child into the classroom to assist the student and teacher.

Grouping
Putting a number of students together to create or evaluate any topic chosen by the teacher. It could be anything from a piece of art work to a science project. Those groups can be homogeneous groups or heterogeneous groups.

Homogenous Groups
The students of the same academic abilities.

Heterogeneous Groups
The students of varied academic abilities - low to high ability.

Peacemakers

A group of students who are trained to direct students to a nonconfrontational method of conflict resolutions. They walk around the playground and direct students where to go for help. These students have good interpersonal skills and are selected to be trained to intercept problems in the playground at recess. They don't solve problems or discipline offenders.

Behavior Deficit

This is a behavior that is harmful and inappropriate in a school setting. Students who display a behavior deficit often get into fights and cause constant turmoil to others. A behavior deficit child needs to be observed, and inappropriate behaviors monitored and modified. An instructional assistant is sometimes assigned to such a child.

Modified Behavior Program

This is a contract or plan whereby a student must guide his/her behavior according to a set plan. Consequences are put in place to offset inappropriate behavior.

Ungrading or Multiage Grouping

When three or more grades are put together in one classroom and taught by one teacher. e.g. grade one, two and three. (Each school setting has a philosophy that goes along with the multiage groupings.)

Split Grade

When two grades are put together in one class and taught by one teacher. (Again, each school has its own philosophy and/or reasons for split grade.)

Integrated Learning

Combining more than one subject area in a lesson or theme. For example, students using the "General Store" theme, do Math by buying and selling. Stories are written about the lives of customers who come to the store. Spelling words are taken from the "General Store" theme. The history of the General Store is studied, and the pioneer's role in it. There is a wealth of possibilities based on the teacher's creativity!

Anecdotal Report

Written comments from teachers gained by observation of the student's academic and social performance.

Attention Deficit
A child who has a great deal of difficulty attending to his/her assignments in school. Any task put before a child like this would take a long time to complete. This child's attention span would be very limited. Easily distracted, a child with attention deficit would have difficulty concentrating on the task at hand.

Child Centered Learning
Students learn by the child's involvement in all aspects of learning. Students interact with other students. It is generally a hands on experimental type of learning.

Individualized Learning
Here a student's learning program is designed specifically for the individualized student. It is not designed for a group. The student's skill level, ability level, learning style, etc. should be taken into consideration.

Activity Based Learning
Here students learn the concepts in any subject area through activities. They would use manipulatives in math, experiment in science, and use hands on activities that promote exploration.

Brainstorming
A cliché term that sets students wondering about the topic at hand. Students come up with multiple possibilities considering the problem at hand.

Process Thinking
This is thinking based on the process skills that initiate better, more effective thinking levels. They are knowledge, comprehension, application, analysis, synthesis, and evaluation as outlined in Bloom's Taxonomy.

Creative Problem Solving
CPS is where students learn a problem solving technique such as the Cort Method, the Parnes Problem Solving Technique, etc. CPS causes students to defer their judgments until they have examined all aspects of the problem.

Manipulatives
Students using blocks, geometric shapes and different materials to learn math concepts.

Summative Report

The use of marks to evaluate the student's academic progress.

Co-operative Learning

This is co-operative small group learning that allows students to interact with and learn from one another as well as from the teacher. The students are encouraged to build on one another's ideas and experiences to learn more effectively. Interaction and discussion are usually achieved through groups of four or five students. The groupings are generally heterogeneous and based on ethnicity, gender, personality and ability. There is usually a communicator, a manager, a tracker, a checker, and a coach.

Metacognition

This term is used by educational theorists. It simply means 'how to think about your thinking processes'. It is the analysis about the whole realm and structure of an individual's thinking processes.

Resource Based Learning

Students, teachers and librarians work together to insure that a large range of library materials and resources are utilized in research. This includes print and non-print materials.

CHAPTER 4

Decoding Your Child's Report Card

The following phrases provide parents with a translation of the teacher jargon so widely used in report cards. At times teachers are in a quandary, wondering how to communicate what they really mean to say to the parent. It isn't easy to put something down in writing because it stays with the child throughout his/her school experience. Parents need to know what the teacher means. Sometimes this proves to be difficult when dealing with a wide spectrum of personalities.

There are basically three parent types:

1.   Parents who hang on every word the teacher says. The parent takes the advice / recommendations and apply them to their child's learning practices as best they can. This type of parent does not usually question what the teacher is doing.

2.   Parents who question everything the teacher says and wonders why and how the teacher arrives at these conclusions...even after it has been explained.

3.   Parents who would like to make sure their child is achieving and developing to his/her greatest personal potential. These parents would like to become more educated in determining how their child is performing socially and academically compared to what is referred to as "the norm". They want to support the school but they also want to make sure the school setting is providing the appropriate academic instruction and social setting for their child.

Here are phrases commonly used on report cards. I have attempted to decipher what they really mean and suggest follow up questions parents could ask.

Phrase:
    "Your child is working to his greatest potential".

Decode:
> *Your child is probably doing the very best he/she can at whatever level she is working at.*

Parents Should Ask:
> What is my child's greatest potential? Is he/she working at grade level? How do you know? How was this potential answered?

Phrase:
> **Joel has the ability to be an excellent student, however outside distractions often divert his attention.**

Decode:
> *Joel is fooling around in the classroom and is causing discipline problems even though he is bright and capable of achieving a high academic standard. He is far more social than he should be during class time! This is causing him to miss assignments, do messy disorganized work, or complete the bare minimum requirements to get the work finished.*

Parents Should Ask:
> Is my bright child being challenged in the higher levels of thinking? Can he be challenged so he is not bored? How can I help you make him take his work seriously to empower him to do his best?

Phrase:
> **Arthur has improved greatly this term. However he still has to put more time and effort into his work.**

Decode:
> *Arthur is probably easily distracted in school. Improving greatly means he probably is not doing some of the things he used to, but needs to focus on his work. The fact that he needs to put more time into his work, makes me wonder how far behind he is.*

Parents Should Ask:
> What exactly is Arthur's behavior in class? How does he disrupt? What do you mean by more time and effort into his work? How much time is he putting into it right now? How can we reinforce his positive behavior? What caused his improvement this term? How can we build on that? How far behind in his work is he?

Phrase:
> **Mark is a delight in class! His assignments are completed**

on time. More attention to neat work would enable Mark's grades to increase.

Decode:

Mark is not making sure his assignments are neatly organized and well thought out. He is accomplishing the work just as quickly as he can to get assignments in on time.

Parents Should Ask:

May I see examples of his assignments? Is he required to recopy messy assignments?

Phrase:

Lisa is doing very well this term. Keep up the good work!

Decode:

Lisa is handing in her homework, and doing well in the teacher's evaluation of her.

Parents Should Ask:

What does "doing very well" mean? What tests have been given to her? How do you evaluate her? If she's doing very well, what kind of enrichment program is given to her? How is her thinking ability being extended in the classroom?

The above phrases are the kind of "open-ended" comments teachers are often required to make on report cards. It is up to parents to demand specific marks of their child's progress if that is what they want. Some parents are content with the "feel good" phrases. Others want more specific information. They are entitled to it.

If parents are dissatisfied with the reporting system employed by the school their child is attending, they should voice these concerns to the teachers and the Principal.

Parents should know exactly where their child stands academically in every subject area. Parents should have input into how this should happen.

CHAPTER 5

What To Do When There Are Problems At School

There is nothing more unsettling to a parent than when a problem arises at school and it seems impossible to resolve! There are times when personality conflicts and frustration can cause havoc! Parents often feel intimidated if the school is not providing the academic and social support the parent expects.

These are situations where parents sometimes approach teachers and principals in an inappropriate manner. This places both parties in jeopardy.

What to do when there is a problem with your child in school.

Step 1: Go to the teacher, explain the problem.
Step 2: Map out a plan to empower your child to learn. Work as a team with the school teachers. You and the teacher should support this plan to make it work.

What to do when problems cannot be resolved between you, your child and the teacher.

Meet with the teacher and the principal - all together - to discuss the problem again. Try to work as a team to empower your child to learn. If there is a conflict or misunderstanding between your child, the teacher or the principal, try to resolve it. The only interest the parties involved should have, should be in the well being and education of your child.

Other resources to go to if problems cannot be worked out at the school level.

Every School Division has a Superintendent and Assistant Superintendents who are in charge of all concerns in regards to the education of your child. When conflicts cannot be resolved, contact the Board Office in your School Division. Find out who you should talk to concerning the problem. You will likely be referred to an Assistant Superintendent. Try to resolve the problem there. If this does not happen, the next course is to go directly to the Superintendent.

You have elected officials of the Board who hold meetings on a monthly basis. Problems concerning the implementation of new programs and policies are ultimately dealt with at the Board level. Find out who the Chairperson of the Board is and relate your concerns. These elected officials are mandated to reflect the concerns, wants and needs of the tax payers who elected them to office. Be aware of this.

School systems are set up in such a way to enable parents to acquire the education their children need to become productive members of society.

1st Link in Chain
CLASSROOM SETTING - TEACHER / CHILD RELATIONSHIP

This is where most problems are resolved. Parents should first deal with the classroom teacher. Explain the concerns in detail. Set up strategies where the teacher and parent work together to help the child.

2nd Link in Chain
THE PRINCIPAL

When serious concerns about a child's academic progress arise and cannot be resolved within the classroom with the child's teacher, it is time to contact the Principal. Many Principals have a wide and varied experience dealing with teachers and parents. Conflict situations and parental concerns need to be resolved to help the learning situation. Parents have a right to voice their concerns. The school is there to give your child his/her best possible education.

3rd Link in Chain
THE SUPERINTENDENT

Parents can phone their local School Division Offices and make an appointment to see the Superintendent. If a School Division is very large there are times the parent will be referred to an Assistant Superintendent. If this occurs, and the problem is not resolved, the parent should insist on meeting with the Superintendent.

4th Link in Chain
THE SCHOOL BOARD OF TRUSTEES

The School Board of Trustees are elected officials. They endorse educational programs, pass policies and are supposed to reflect the wishes of their constituents. When parents have a concern, they can present their concerns at a public forum. The School Boards have meetings on a monthly basis and parents can be put on the agenda and voice their concerns about the educational system through this medium.

Also, they can phone their School Division office and get the name and phone number of their elected trustees. This enables parents to contact trustees and speak with then on a personal level.

CHAPTER 6

How To Recognize Good Teaching Practices

Teachers should be incorporating Lower to Higher Level Thinking Skills, Process Thinking Skills and Creative Problem Solving to every unit of work taught in the classroom. This is true for grades K-12.

The **Thinking Levels** provide experiences from the easiest to the more complex. The **Processes** cause students to apply their thinking skills to activity based learning. These skills supply the students with specific methods of applying their learning to scientific inquiry. Learning **Creative Problem Solving** helps the students defer their judgments until examination of all aspects of the problem is complete.

The **synthesis** of the **Thinking Levels, Process Thinking** and **Creative Problem Solving** is an indication that good teaching practices are in place for your child.

The Synthesis

These components are developed from a synthesis of many educational ideas. Its three basic components are:

Bloom's Cognitive Thinking Levels - Knowledge, Comprehension, Application, Analysis, Synthesis, Evaluation.

Science Process Skills - Observing, Classifying, Measuring and Use of Number Communicating, Inferring, Predicting, Interpreting Data, Hypothesizing and Controlling Variables.

Creative Problem Solving -
Level 1 - Sensing Problems and Challenges
Level 2 - Fact Finding
Level 3 - Problem Finding
Level 4 - Idea Finding
Level 5 - Solution Finding
Level 6 - Acceptance Finding

#1 - Bloom's Cognitive Levels

Bloom's development of the taxonomy of educational objectives helped curriculum planners and evaluators in their work but the impact of Bloom's work failed to reach the classroom teacher for many years. Some teachers in the last few years have found it helpful to use these categories of objectives as an aid to planning and teaching. Bloom's taxonomy of cognitive objectives is an attempt to indicate the various levels of thinking on which the instructional objectives are based. The taxonomy describes a hierarchy of intellectual process from basic knowledge through comprehension, application, analysis, synthesis and evaluation. The lowest level objectives can be achieved by memorization and the hierarchy progresses as the type of learning becomes more complex. The following list adapted from Simpson and Anderson (1980) summarizes the cognitive domain. This list is still widely used as a basis for thinking levels in school. (See Figure 1 & 2)

Knowledge
To be able to recall information, such as specifics, methods, processes or patterns. Verbs used may be chooses, defines, identifies, labels, lists, describes, states.

Comprehension
To know what is being communicated and to be able to understand the concepts involved. Verbs used are explains, summarizes, give examples, distinguishes, compare, contrast.

Application
To use knowledge in concrete situations. Verbs used are demonstrate, discover, solve, use, modify, predict.

Analysis
To break down information into its parts or elements. Verbs used are distinguish, discriminate, illustrate, analyze, test, infer.

Synthesis
To put together elements or parts so as to form a whole. Verbs used are hypothesize, design, revise, compose, collect, formulate.

Evaluation
To make judgments using criteria or standards. Verbs used are appraise, criticize, interpret, choose, evaluate.

BLOOM'S LEARNING TAXONOMY

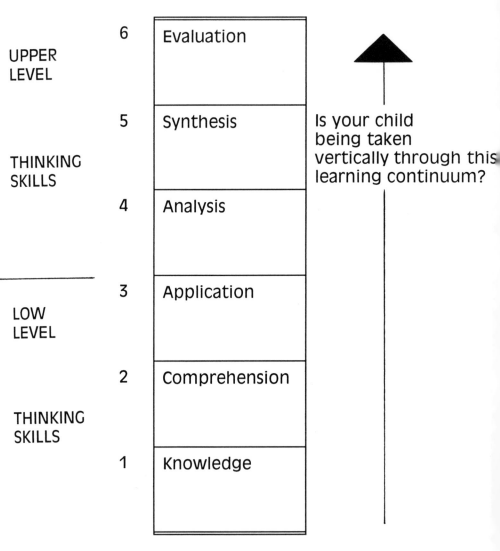

FIGURE 1

A REFERENCE FOR PARENTS

"THE THREE LITTLE PIGS"

LEVEL 6	Evaluation	1. **Critique** the lifestyles of each pig. 2. **Determine** the wolf's lung capacity by **measuring** the "air" force required to move straw, wood and brick.
LEVEL 5	Synthesis	1. **Create** a 'straw' brick and test it for strength. Begin with a 1:1 ratio of straw to mud, or plaster, etc. 2. **Write** 5 **new** chants for the wolf and 5 new corresponding responses from the pigs.
LEVEL 4	Analysis	1. **Diagram** an overhead view of where the pigs and the wolf live and the route the wolf took to their homes. 2. **Break** the countries of the world **into** 2 **parts**: those who have a "wolf at the door," and those which do not.
LEVEL 3	Application	1. **Predict** what the wolf could do next, in order to enter the third pig's home. 2. **Classify** types of shelter today according to: a) strawlike b) woodlike c) bricklike
LEVEL 2	Comprehension	1. **Explain** why the straw house was easily destroyed. 2. **Contrast** and **compare** the pigs' 3 homes.
LEVEL 1	Knowledge	1. **Name** the 3 types of homes which the pigs built. 2. **Recite** or **quote** the wolf's warning to the pigs.

FIGURE 2 Bloom's Taxonomy With Sample Questions, Using The Three Little Pigs As a Reference

2 - Science Process Skills

These process skills are the basic elements of the **scientific** approach to thinking. Children need to be taught them in the context of science lessons. They then proceed in a systematic way from the basic skills to the integrated skills.

Problem Finding
The ability to wonder about something which requires an answer through experimentation and data collection.

Observing
The use of our five senses, in combination with measuring, to describe objects and events. Our five senses are hearing, seeing, smelling, tasting and touching.

Classifying
Sorting or ordering objects, ideas, or events, according to their properties (i.e. similarities and differences)

Measuring and Use of Number
Making more precise statements about data by means of standard and non-standard units and other quantifying conventions, including proper use of instruments.

Predicting
Forecasting made about future events based upon data already obtained. Includes interpolation and extrapolation.

Interpreting Data
Using and selecting data to draw inferences, determine relationships, identify trends, or state conclusions.

Inferring
Suggesting more about a set of conditions than is observed; i.e. a guess based upon experience plus observation.

Hypothesizing
Suggesting the relationships between the factors studied.

Experimenting
Designing experiments based on problems which students decide need to be resolved.

Communicating
The use of appropriate means to communicate scientific information, including models, maps, graphs, data tables; in addition to oral and written methods. Note: This process is used at all levels.

3 - Creative Problem Solving

There are Creative Problem Solving Techniques that are widely used across North America. The one following is a modified method designed by Parnes (1972). Every teacher should know a Creative Problem Solving Technique and apply it to their teaching practices.
The basic idea of CPS is to cause students to defer their solutions to a problem until they have explored all the aspects of the problem. Very good thinkers are very good problem solvers because they have the ability to see all the connections.

Level 1 - Sensing Problems and Challenges
This involves an awareness of problems needed to be solved. The purpose of participating in this level is to enable children to name and describe situations in need of improvement.

Level 2 - Fact Finding
It is a process of guided scientific inquiry basic to understanding why a problem exists. The students are encouraged to *ask* Who? What? Where? Why? and How? relative to the problem.

Level 3 - Problem Finding
Here the facts are reviewed and a problem search is conducted which could produce many mini-problems. These are mini-problems that occur because of the major problems. Students **must not try to solve** any of the mini-problems. It is a technique for opening up their brain power. This helps them to solve the major problems by looking at all aspects.

Level 4 - Idea Finding
This involves a great deal of divergent thinking. Brainstorming techniques are encouraged to help students produce a number of original ideas. Students are encouraged to be non-judgmental while ideas are being elaborated.

Level 5 - Solution Finding
Here students are encouraged to evaluate the many ideas

generated in level four. They are taught to look at their ideas realistically while remaining emotionally at distance from them. They must produce data to support their choice - a solution that has the best chance of succeeding. This choice must be made from the list of ideas for solutions presented in level four.

Level 6 - Acceptance Finding

Here the student goes beyond solving the problem to finding ways of implementing the solution to the problem. It is not enough to "solve" a problem. The solution must make sense and possibly become a reality.

Some students and adults have the ability to problem solve and think in the higher levels because they were born with a given ability or talent.

These people see relationships and make connections readily. Learning a problem solving technique helps these people to apply their abilities in a more meaningful manner.

There is a Problem Solving Institute at the State University in Buffalo New York. A conference is held the last week of June every year. Many teachers, business people and politicians find it worthwhile to attend these conferences. Problem Solving is of paramount importance in this day and age.

Prior to the teaching of any unit, or concept to children, parents and teachers need to find out what the child thinks about it. Two well known theorists called Ausubel and Novak said that educators need to build on what students already know and understand. The newest theory used in the teaching of science is constructivism. Constructivists say that in order for meaningful learning to occur, prior experiences have to be discussed to understand what the child knows or believes about the concept to be learned.

Children construct their own ideas based on experiences within the context of their own world. Children bring their own ideas to the learning situation - whether these ideas or perceptions are correct or incorrect. Therefore, before any science concept is taught, children need to discuss, brainstorm and share their ideas. Parents should be aware of this so they can support their children's learning at school.

After learning new ideas, children should be able to apply their new knowledge to real world situations. They need time to reflect on their learning as well. Parents can recognize good teaching practices when this type of teaching takes place.

Good units of learning takes the learning beyond the realm of memorization and in to the higher order thinking levels.

Good units of learning should have all the thinking levels included as outlined in Bloom's Taxonomy, the Science Process Thinking Skills and the Creative Problem Solving component.

The following lesson plans are excerpts from the TCA Method (Leith and Smith). They are examples of a variety of topics coupled with the mandatory teaching practices.

These are examples of units that teachers design to teach the curriculum. It gives parents some idea of the thinking that should go into these units. Different teachers bring their own style and own teaching methods to each unit of learning. However, parents should question when teachers cannot produce their lesson plans or designs to justify what they are teaching the children.

LESSON 1
Integration of Science, Language Arts and Math

Science Elementary

Theme: Food Chains (Population Interaction)

Objectives:

1. To Teach the Following Process Skills

- Data Gathering
- Classifying
- Interpreting Data
- Making Inferences
- Making Predictions
- Defining Operationally

2. To Give Students Experience in the Following Thinking Levels

- Knowledge - Memorizing Specific bits of information and various bits of knowledge (e.g. which animals are carnivores, herbivores, omnivores, predators and scavengers).

- Comprehension - Understanding the data gathered through the data gathering method, the interpretation of the data and the predictions and inferences made. E.g. what are the characteristics of a herbivore? - that they eat plants, the characteristics of an omnivore? - they eat both plants and animals, the characteristics of a predator? - that they hunt and kill their food, and the characteristics of scavengers who are nature's garbage collectors and do not hunt and kill the animals but clean up the carcasses. Using this conformation the students will grow to understand what makes a food chain happen.

- Application - Applying the newly gathered information to a new situation. Here the students draw their own food situation. Here the students draw their own food chain using a different location and different types of animals (e.g. the students could study the tundra and find out that the caribou are herbivores and eat the lichen on the frozen tundra. The arctic wolf then preys upon the caribou to enable them to exist in the frozen north. In turn, man will hunt the wolf for sport and then enters into the life cycle of the tundra).

- Analysis - Analyzing the data, extrapolating, drawing conclusions. Here the student analyzes all the information he/she has acquired through the understanding of what comprises the various characteristics of the different animal populations in the tundra. Here the students come up with possible problems that might occur in the tundra (e.g. what would happen if the caribou population became too plentiful and all the lichen was eaten).

- Synthesis - Arriving at a solution to a problem arising from the study of the food chain in the tundra. After analyzing the data and coming up with conclusions about problems that might occur in the food cycle in the tundra the student should now arrive at solutions to the problem that they have stated.

- Evaluation - Here the students make judgments about their solutions and decide whether or not their conclusions are reasonable based on the knowledge and understanding they have acquired of their subject area.

3. To Teach Logical Thinking Within The Context of a Creative Problem Solving Technique

- Senses and Challenges - After having studied the specific information and acquired the needed knowledge and factual data about the given subject, the students are then encouraged to state a problem very specifically and state why it is a problem. (e.g. the seals are becoming extinct. It is a problem because it is affecting the polar bear population which depends upon the seals for their food).

- Fact Finding - Students now ask themselves the who? what? where? when? why? and how? questions that surround the stated problem. To enable them to do this they have to study the seals and the polar bear. They also have to know a lot about the ecology and weather conditions in the north.

- Problem Finding - Students brainstorm for all the possible mini problems that may occur because of the major problems. (e.g. they might suggest that because the seals are becoming extinct and the polar bear population is being affected by it, then other animals might run into problems also.)

- Idea Finding - Students brainstorm for all possible solutions to the major problem stated in senses and challenges. Here the student must not get caught up in the mini problems that he or she has listed in problem finding. The mini problems are not the problems that have to be solved but rather are stated to enable the student to open up all possible ways of dealing with the major problem. Here the students are encouraged to be very creative. Far out ideas are encouraged.

- Solution Finding - Students select the best possible solution to the problem by evaluating all possible solutions listed in the idea finding. After they have selected the best possible solution they must state why they think the solution they have selected is the best one.

- Acceptance Finding - Students must find ways to implement the solution. It is not enough to come up with a solution. They must apply the solution to the real world situation and make it workable. It must make sense to them.

Lesson Procedures:
Have students study various food chains and make charts of their observations and conclusions.

Suggested Activities:
Gather data on the various animal populations in the tundra and make graphs.
- have groups of students study the characteristics of the various animal populations in the tundra and make charts classifying these characteristics.
- have students make a collage depicting food chains.

- have students compare and contrast food chains found in different parts of the world (e.g. tundra populations vs. jungle populations).
- observe terrariums and aquariums for food chains.
- construct and label food web organisms as scavengers, decomposers, or predators to show population interactions. Observe playground or wooded areas for food chains and population interactions.
- construct an earthworm farm. Observe and record interactions.
- construct an ant colony to observe home building.
- observe these over a period of days, record data, make inferences and predictions.

NOTE:

It is important for the instructor to keep referring back to the original objectives listed under process skills, thinking levels and creative problem solving skills. Some students will need to study the specific subject area in great depth. Others will need more time to study the specific characteristics of the animal populations to understand what comprises a food chain.

Lesson # 2
Integration of Science, Math and Language Arts

Theme: Electricity

Objectives:

1. To Teach the Following Process Skills

- Defining Operationally
- Data Gathering
- Interpreting Data
- Making Inferences
- Making Predictions

2. To Give Students Experience in the Following Thinking Levels

- Knowledge - Memorizing specific bits of information needed to know about electricity and how circuit boards work.

- Comprehension - Understanding the data gathered through the use of inferences, predictions and the interpretation of the given data.

The students must understand how electricity occurs.

- Application - Applying the gathered information and data to a new situation. After the students have gathered knowledge and understanding of how electricity works, they apply this information to the making of a computer. Here the students can draw diagrams of the electrical circuit.

- Analysis - Here the students analyze their data, extrapolate and draw conclusions.

- Synthesis - The students construct or arrive at a solution to a problem arising from the study of electricity or the making of a circuit board.

- Evaluation - Here the students make judgments about the solution and evaluate their interpretations of their gathered data.

3. To Teach Logical Thinking Within the Context of a Creative Problem Solving Technique

- Senses and Challenges - Have students state a problem about electricity or circuit boards, whichever they choose, and then state why it is a problem, e.g. How could we make a circuit board that would help us with learning our times tables?

- Fact Finding - Students ask the who? what? where? when? why? and how? questions surrounding the stated problem, e.g. who is involved with making the circuit board, what are the materials used in making a circuit board? where will the circuit board be located?, when was the first circuit board made? and how was the circuit board made?

- Problem Finding - Students brainstorm for all the possible mini problems that may occur because of the major problems, e.g. students may not want to learn the times tables by another method, or the circuit board might be hard to carry, or the circuit board light might burn out easily. (Here the students are encouraged to list all kinds of mini problems that might occur as a direct result of the major problem.)

- Idea Finding - Students brainstorm for all the possible solutions to the stated problem in the senses and challenges. Here students are encouraged to be very creative. Far out ideas are encouraged, e.g. all sorts of different types of circuit boards would be created using concepts learned in the making of an electrical circuit.

- Solution Finding - Students select the best possible solution to the problem by evaluating all the possible solutions listed in idea finding. After they have selected the best possible solution, they must state why it is the best solution.

- Acceptance Finding - Students must find ways to implement the solution and make it workable. If they decide to construct a computer to enable them to learn their times tables, it must be a simple enough circuit that indeed students can learn their times tables quickly and efficiently.

Lesson Procedures:
Have students study basic ideas, electricity and make predictions about what will happen when they have constructed their electrical circuits. They must understand that electricity will flow if they have a dry cell with wires attached at the negative and positive terminals. If they connect this to a bulb and construct a switch, electricity should flow. Once they have studied about series and parallel circuits the students will be able to apply this to the making of a circuit board.

Suggested Activities:
Construct a variety of circuit boards using parallel and series circuits. Draw up an advertising campaign "selling" your new computer idea for learning times tables quickly and efficiently. Be a real scientist and do a research project! Try to find out if students learn their times tables faster by rote memory or by using the computer. To do this pick two subjects. Subject A and Subject B. Give Subject A the times tables you want them to learn. Time Subject A and find out exactly how long it took Subject A to learn the times tables by rote memory. Give Subject B the computer and a set of times tables to learn. Time Subject B and record how long it took Subject B to learn the times tables. To make the study more viable, use more subjects (people) and a bigger variety of times tables. Upon gathering the data and interpreting it, the investigator will be able to draw logical conclusions based on his or her study. Make charts classifying the different computers after identifying their particular characteristics.

LESSON # 3
Integration of Science, Math and Language Arts

Theme: PEDESTRIAN CROSSINGS - Real World Problem Solving

Objectives:

1. To Teach the Following Process Skills

- Graphing Skills
- Data Gathering
- Interpretation of Data
- Making Inferences
- Making Predictions
- Classifying

2. To Give Students Experience in the Following Thinking Levels

- Knowledge - Memorizing specific bits of information and various bits of knowledge.

- Comprehension - Understanding the data gathered through the use of inferences and interpretation of data, etc.

- Application - Applying the gathered information and data to a new situation. Drawing diagrams, graphs, etc.

- Analysis - Analyzing the data, extrapolating, drawing conclusions, etc.

- Synthesis - Arriving at a solution to a problem arising from the study of pedestrian crossings.

- Evaluation - Making judgments about the solution, evaluating the procedures for gathering data.

3. To Teach Logical Thinking Within the Context of a Creative Problem Solving Technique

- Senses and Challenges - Have students state a problem about the Pedestrian Crossing and why it is a problem.

43

- Fact Finding - Students ask who? what? where? when? why? and how? questions surrounding the stated problem.

- Problem Finding - Students brainstorm for all the possible mini problems that may occur because of the major problems.

- Idea Finding - Students brainstorm for all the possible solutions to the major problem stated in Senses and Challenges. Here students are encouraged to be very creative and far out ideas are encouraged.

- Solution Finding - Students select the best possible solution to the problem by evaluating all the possible solutions listed in Idea Finding. After they have selected the best possible solution they must write down why they think it is the best possible solution.

- Acceptance Finding - Students must find ways to implement the solution. It is not enough to come up with a solution - they must apply this solution to the real world situation and make it workable.

Lesson Procedure:
   Students observe the Pedestrian Crossings around their school, making lists and charts of their observations. (They could classify their observations under Hazard and Non-Hazard).

Suggested Activities:
- Record number of pedestrians crossing at the pedestrian crossing areas around the school at busy times and at less busy times.
- Time how long it takes various students to cross the pedestrian crosswalk. Make predictions about how long it will take an individual to cross. Make inferences as to why it takes some students longer than others to cross at the pedestrian crosswalks.
- Make observations about the safety signs.
- List ways to make the pedestrian crosswalks safer.
- Have students draw maps of the area around the pedestrian crossings.
- Measure the distance across each crosswalk.
- Make charts classifying the various kinds of vehicles that pass by the pedestrian crossings.
- Make up a jingle, poem, song or story promoting safety around crosswalks.
- Write letters to the local politicians to make them aware of any

hazard to the safety of pedestrians due to lack of safety signs, flashing lights, patrols, etc.

- Organize a safety campaign in the school to make the students more aware of the dangers at pedestrian crossings.

NOTE:

It is important that the instructor keeps referring back to the original objectives listed under Process Skills, Thinking levels and Creative Problem Solving Skills. The students in the regular classroom can make observations about the pedestrian crossings. However, some students will remain in the easier process of observation while others will progress to the more difficult processes of making inferences and interpreting data. Also some students will remain longer in the knowledge, comprehension levels of thinking while others progress through the application analysis and synthesis levels of thinking. The same is true for the creative problem solving. Some students will remain longer at Senses and Challenges level while the more able student will process rapidly through all levels. Each student should be treated as an individual and allowed to grow at his/her own rate according to the particular level of cognitive development the student is at. That is why it is helpful for the instructor to write down the various activities the students progress through on a daily basis.

CHAPTER 7

Mathematics!
Why Can't My Child Learn It?
(and how does problem solving tie into it?)

When students are asked which subject causes them the most trouble and/or boredom, they are most likely to reply "either math or science". Unfortunately, we as parents sometimes eagerly volunteer this information: "I was never good in math, either". Why do our sons, our daughters and we ourselves begin to have more and more trouble in math as the school years march by? It's partly because math is an exact science. Precise value, data, and processes must be adhered to whether we're using a formula to find area or solving a word problem. Math information also accumulates and builds on itself gradually (and I do mean gradually) up until grade nine. From grade nine to twelve it seems the math flood gates have been opened - algebra, calculus, trigonometry and physics. No longer is simple recall of a math fact good enough. Now the student who was just getting a grip on that area, formula, or multiplication fact must learn even more math principles and apply them at an analysis and synthesis level! In other words - Problem Solving. This requires mental discipline, a skill, even a patience, we are not teaching our children very well. It is no accident that enrollment in physics and math continues to drop while many students will opt for biology. The difference again is simple. The former requires more upper level thinking, success in the latter depends mostly on recall - knowledge, comprehension - low level thinking.

So how can you as parents help your children to overcome this math anxiety? A major step in the right direction is a thinking skills program. Schools should be formally teaching children to think and one arm of any thinking skills program should be the deliberate and direct teaching of the steps involved in good problem solving. Secondly, schools and homes must continuously foster a positive attitude towards math, a desire to become a good thinker, a will to change the way we view problem solving, a pride in accuracy and a correct solution.

Problem solving is a process integral to Mathematics. Students who acquire a thorough knowledge of problem solving techniques

become much better math problem solvers.

Here are some things to watch for in a good problem solving program.

One

Most importantly, specific thinking skills necessary for problem solving should be taught directly, modeled and assessed.

It is not enough to pass out questions requiring 'problem solving' and 'hope' that each child employs necessary skills. Neither is it enough to wave documents about proclaiming the benefits of such skills.

Barry K. Beyer, one of the foremost authorities on developing thinking skills programs describes it this way: "Learning to think is not the incidental outcome of the classroom study of diverse subjects. Nor is it the result of simply responding to teacher or textbook questions. Being willing and able to engage in skillful, effective thinking requires, instead, purposeful learning of how to execute the procedures used in decision making, problem solving, and other major thinking tasks."[2]

Beyer goes on to say: "To improve the quality of student thinking as much as we can, we must turn to teaching directly the skills and strategies that constitute thinking. Such teaching has three dimensions: it makes thinking skills and strategies the subject of instruction, the substance to be learned. It focuses explicitly on the attributes of the skills and strategies being taught; and it employs techniques of direct instruction".[3]

Two

Problem solving should be operationally defined by the school. A math problem solving program, should be scope and sequenced - and its objectives, methods, goals together with a time line clearly set out.

Several researchers have defined problem solving in great detail, including Beyer. At a glance it includes many important thinking skills - generalizing, hypothesis testing, detailed analysis, common knowledge and accuracy to name some. Arthur Whimbey and Jack Lockhead have come at it another way.[4] Their research has uncovered the 24 most common errors in reasoning, practiced by problem solvers. Through vocalization of actual problem solving the solver learns skills to overcome these errors.[5] The point is, there is valuable research and ideas out there on how to teach our children to think. Let's start building on some of it! Let's become academic about academics! Parents should know that mathematical basics need to be taught and applied to problems.

Three

A sound purposeful problem solving program should not depend solely on recurring mention of the term "problem solving".

Education is filled with terms and they can be dangerous because just the mere mention of them does not an academic program make. While speaking at the 1991 National Institute in Winnipeg, Dr. Willard R. Daggett, Director of the International Center for Leadership in Education - New York, referred to the abuse and misuse of 'terms'. As an example he asked, "Problem solving and decision making - do we teach them? No. Most teachers don't even know the difference between the two".[6] This is relevant for any subject area, Math or otherwise.

Four

A good problem solving program relies partly on the vocalization of problem solving skills. The solver should be able to orally describe the skills and steps he/she is mentally experiencing.

This articulation and deliberate manipulation of steps of some or all thinking processes is called metacognition. A simple definition of metacognition is 'thinking about your thinking'.

This brings us back to the use of 'terms', like problem solving. Simply affording students a chance to practice their problem solving by handing out problems or work sheets, or pointing to the curriculum, which says teach more problem solving, is not the teaching of the processes and skills found in problem solving - a major and complex cognitive operation.

Five

A good problem solving program should demonstrate and encourage the transfer of problem solving skills to many subject areas, not just math.

In other words the problem solving encountered when writing an essay is in many ways similar to solving a mathematical word problem and/or a verbal reasoning problem. An explanation of the broader use of problem skills should act as a motivation to many weak and average students. It crosses all curricular boundaries and deters students from cornering themselves with self defeating statements like "I love science but I'm lousy in math".

Six

A good problem solving program actively pursues accuracy, as a distinct goal in itself.

Quite simply, 'accuracy' is the mind deliberately and intensely focusing its attention on the correctness of each step in a problem solving process, not just at the end. The solver wants to solve the problem the right way, the best way. However, this contrasts with a disturbing attitude found in many students today - "I just don't care if I get the right answer".

In its metacognitive form a good problem solver would constantly interrupt his ongoing thinking processes for a split second, with inquiries like: "...was that last answer correct?", "Does that make sense?" and "...do I usually make a mistake with this type of information?"

In their research on problem solving, Whimbey and Lockhead directly address the teaching of accuracy: "...errors are primarily caused by lack of accuracy and thoroughness in thinking. Research has shown that accuracy and thoroughness are mental habits which can be cultivated through training and exercise".[7]

Seven

A good problem solving program incorporates some form of evaluation.

This could be a combination of standardized tests, school made tests, personal observation, peer consultation and the recording of students thinking aloud as they solve problems. This last method is an exciting technique recommended by many experts in the field of thinking skills. It promotes individualized learning and offers a detailed look at each student's metacognitive processes.

It is very important that a school decide on some method of evaluation. The school must have goals for its problem solving program and these goals must be tested. To do otherwise is to pretend, to hope that the program is significantly changing the academic abilities of most students. If businesses operated this way, they wouldn't last long! So parents should be asking, "Has ungrading significantly raised math marks, or is everything in the school just 'wonderful' due to ungrading?" It doesn't have to be ungrading. The same question applies to child centered learning, whole language, co-operative learning, or any other initiative.

Eight

A good problem solving program should stimulate school dynamics, and school dynamics should stimulate widespread interest in problem solving.

School dynamics is a positive energy in the school. The staff is enthusiastic and the majority of students are happy, challenged, and aware that they are being challenged (taken care of) - that people and programs are there to improve them. A warning: the excitement (positive energy) does not center solely around school teas, Christmas pageants and visiting authors, or hot dog days, (although these are necessary to a school). The excitement should also focus on academics, new programs to improve academic standards.

The school should be alive and expectations in years ahead should be for higher standards. They are not 'hoped' for, they are purposefully striven for!

When asked, students can describe what the academic goals of the school are, what special programs are offered. Activities build on each other and should range all the way from a detailed scope and sequence, (not mission statements) stringent yet growth producing, to school T-shirts exhorting the power of thinking and problem solving! Math problem solving should be valued, not feared by the students.

Questions and Answers About Math

Does your child's teacher say that math drill is now a thing of the past?

I don't know of too many skills that do not require practice. I say practice because that's what a drill is - practice. Whether it's the rites of spring for children - soccer and baseball, or learning to play a musical instrument or even raising your score in a video game - repeated practice is essential! Just for a moment can you imagine your 13 year old son saying to the hockey coach, "Coach, I'm not attending any more practices". So YES, drill is important. Don't be drawn in by a new 'feel good' philosophy which likens drill to an ancient barbaric ritual. Teachers can and do make such routines interesting, challenging and even fun.

Our school is now saying that the use of calculators and estimation skills make drill and basic math skills less important, even obsolete. Is this so?

You have to tread carefully here, for your child's benefit. Estimation has always been an important skill. Adults use it all the time. It is a skill requiring basic math, some generalizing skills and even good visual imagery skills. But in math, it still necessitates some mental arithmetic and this means math basics. For example to estimate the cost of 79 dresses at $67 each, does the mind still not have to know the answer to 80 x 70, or more precisely the 7 times tables? The calculator is a useful tool, but the amount of use it gets should be in direct correlation to the child's proficiency with basic skills. In my opinion, the average elementary or middle years student who has not bothered to learn the basics, has no business relying on a calculator.

Does your child possess common knowledge?

We all carry around varying amounts of knowledge in our heads, some greater, some less, dependent on what field of endeavor we're involved. However, some knowledge is so basic or common to school, that without it, math problem solving is nearly impossible in some cases. Here is a sample of facts which always hinder students: how many days in a year? how many weeks in a year? which months have 30 days, how many meters in a kilometer? how many years in a decade? how many degrees in a circle? how many centimeters in a meter? how many minutes is a quarter of an hour? how to tell time from a clock face? how much time passes between any two given times? You can keep adding to this list. It takes only a bit of practice in extra math classes and a small amount of commitment to acquire these valuable stepping stones. Your child should know these things.

Does your child seem to be covering topics in math based on the months of the year? In other words, "If it's November, it must be division".

This segmented approach to math does not permit or recognize the need for constant review of previously "learned" skills. The potential for forgetting math skills far exceeds the potential for remembering. Good teachers see to it that math skills are recurrent throughout the week, never mind the month or year. They may not even call it "review". However, your child's math should reflect constant review of previously learned concepts.

Are critical thinking and problem solving the same thing?

NO, definitely not. Beyer describes it this way: "In sum, critical thinking is essentially evaluative in nature. It involves precise, persistent and objective analysis of any claim, source or belief to judge its accuracy, validity and worth.

Unlike problem solving, decision making, or other level one operations, critical thinking is not a strategy. It does not consist of a sequence of operations and subordinate procedures through which one proceeds in generally sequential fashion. Instead, critical thinking is a collection of specific operations that may be used simply or in any combination or in any order".[8] Beyer himself attaches ten major thinking operations to effective critical thinking.

Another well known educator and researcher in the field of the direct teaching of thinking skills, Dr. Deborah E. Burns, places critical thinking skills among six major cognitive operations, and assigns no less than fifteen sub-skills to it in her taxonomy of thinking skills.[9]

So what's the message for parents here? Simply that schools shouldn't be allowed to say they are teaching either cognitive operation without adhering to an accountable guideline. Writing a school paper never implied critical thinking skills ten years ago. So why suddenly is the misused term popping up now in conjunction with a myriad of normal school activities? Next time you hear either term being bandied about by an administrator or trustee, ask for a pedagogical definition of the term, and a copy of the scope and sequenced program used for its implementation!

Why do math text books seem to go over and over the same thing each year?

Some amount of review is helpful and most necessary. But the amount of new knowledge found in text books is in steady decline. Research has shown that from grades K to 8 there is a decrease in new knowledge from 100% in kindergarten/grade one to an average low of 30% new information in grade eight texts. In grade nine it typically surges back to 90%. The new content is due mainly to algebra.

Many provincial and state curriculums have recently been revised to incorporate a more relevant and broader range of math skills. For example, simple algebra instruction now begins in grade five, along with more emphasis on patterns, geometry, estimation, data management and problem solving. Now all we have to do is add one catalyst to the mix, and that's a change In attitude on the part of educators and students.

Should my child practice mental arithmetic at home and at school?

YES, this is a terrific mental exercise, great for visual imagery and provides a real strength in mathematics! Without pencil or paper, *students figure answers in their heads. Good teachers have been practicing it with their classes for years. Above average students use it almost intrinsically. It can take the form of something as simple as a number sequence: count by 7's, 70's or 700's, to a basic multiplication skill: 89x6, to a level three problem: what is the total length of the edges of a box 2m x 2m x 2m?*

Should I be encouraged or discouraged by a 'back to basics' movement in math?

'Back to basics' should be distinguished from 'back to just basics'. No parent wants their child taught just basics in a regimented 1950's style classroom. On the other hand, I think those who realistically and assertively advocate 'back to basics' really want some basic knowledge to stick in their children's heads and therefore act as a springboard to some higher level thinking. Referring to Bloom's Taxonomy, 'basics' can be substituted for the knowledge level, allowing doors to open more easily at the analysis and synthesis levels. In other words parents have quickly realized that their daughter can't solve math problems because their daughter doesn't even know her math basics.

In its broadest sense 'basics' almost surely includes accountability and discipline. There is no simpler or more basic truth than a low mark on a test. There is no simpler or basic lie than to be told that the student can't be taught anymore or any differently, that he/she will "come around" eventually, and gradually come to understanding of the concept.

Should I feel comforted at the recent attention paid to Math and Math problem solving by the education community in general?

*It's a beginning, but the mere mention of the term "new curriculum" will not remedy the situation. Don't forget that the troubles in Math have been evident for eight to ten years now. Departments of Education, administrators and schools are late in addressing the problem. As a parent, you should hold schools to a time line on change that stems from a new curriculum. You can't wait ten **more** years for improved test results!*

CHAPTER 8

Filling The Holes In Whole Language

The past decade has ushered in the advent of a new approach in language arts - Whole Language. This approach is expected to cover the four strands - reading, writing, speaking and listening.

Whole language emphasizes a student centered non standardized approach....the "feel good" approach. Spelling, punctuation, grammar, writing with meaning, decoding with phonics, are not a part of a whole language process. These components are presumed to evolve as the child works with language through the four strands.

The whole language approach frees the teacher up to become more creative with genre and themes. Unfortunately, lack of structure in the whole language approach left children with inconsistent mastery levels in the mechanics of writing and reading.

Parents should make mental checklists concerning their child's writing. There are questions they can ask, and observations they can make, that will give them some idea of how their children are doing.

Parents can know what writing skills their children are receiving by using the following guideline. The following is a checklist parents can use to find out if the writing program is one employing teaching practices which teach your child how to write. Circle yes or no.

In your child's Language Arts program:

1. Is journal writing a part of your child's writing program?

    Yes   No

2. Is the importance of phonics downplayed by your son's teacher or school?

    Yes   No

3. Is your son/daughter often asked to "write something" without any specific writing instruction related to form or process?

    Yes   No

4. Is your middle years child simply asked to complete bulk writing assignments or to write and hand in some of the following writing activities by a certain date?
   - a journal
   - a biography
   - a friendly letter
   - a business letter
   - a poem
   - a joke
   - a news article
   - a descriptive passage
   - a menu
   - a story
   - an anecdote
   - a diary

   Yes   No

5. Is your son/daughter simply asked to *do* some creative writing. For example, instruction would resemble: "Pretend you're on a deserted island. Now write a story about it".

   Yes   No

6. Does your child's writing and reading program frequently depend on random world events in the newspaper? For example: hurricanes.

   Yes   No

7. Does your elementary child practice the sentence only? E.g. A complete sentence is the goal of the Language Arts program.

   Yes   No

8. Does your middle years child practice the paragraph only? E.g. Writing complete paragraphs is the goal of the Language Arts program.

   Yes   No

9. Does your middle years or high school child spend most of the year reading and writing fiction, with very little expository writing or reading for information?

   Yes   No

10. Is the instruction in fiction summed up by:

Introduction, Rising Action, Climax, Falling Action and Conclusion?

Yes   No

11. Is your child's writing graded and edited by other students, not the teacher?

Yes   No

12. Does your son/daughter's teacher often use this expression during interviews, public meetings or daily classes? "I'd rather be the guide on the side, than the sage on the stage."

Yes   No

13. Are your son's / daughter's writing assignments assessed with only a letter grade or brief general comments such as "good work", "nice story", "well done", etc.?

Yes   No

14. Are most of the teacher's anecdotal comments grammatically based? E.g. Good sentence structure, too many run on sentences, no punctuation, etc.

Yes   No

15. Is grammar formally taught?

Yes   No

16. Is spelling formally taught?

Yes   No

17. Does your son/daughter know the difference between expository and narrative writing?

Yes   No

18. Does your middle years son/daughter spend at least 50% of his/her time on expository writing? E.g. Essays

Yes   No

19. Does your middle years and senior years son/daughter actively read and study other authors' essays?

Yes   No

20. Is your child taught rhetorical patterns skills and analysis skills for

their identification and implementation?

Yes   No

21. Is Bloom's Taxonomy used as a continuum for gauging the complexity of writing and reading assignments?

Yes   No

22. Do writing assignment grades appear on the report card?

Yes   No

23. Does your child's middle years or high school teacher write essays or fiction?

Yes   No

The preceding questions are intended as a general guideline and a first step for parents who want to begin taking a closer look at their child's Language Arts program. Language Arts is a sprawling discipline, and one that integrates with all other subject areas. Success in this discipline is crucial. Why? Because every writing assignment is a problem to be solved. Unlike Math though, the answer does not have to be exact. And there lies the enormous loop hole. As a matter of fact if you refer to Bloom's Taxonomy, writing assignments can be called complete and yet be written at a low level of thinking - knowledge, comprehension and application. Where on the continuum does your child normally complete his/her writing tasks? Is it in the upper or lower thinking levels?

Parents are usually (maybe automatically) content just to know that their son or daughter is reading something and writing something. Instead parents should begin to wonder at what level are their sons and daughters reading and writing. Dr. Willard R. Daggett sees this as one of the major short comings in North American education. One of his principle findings is that 75% of workers never use reading and writing for personal response (pleasure). On the contrary, the most common use of both strands today is reading and writing for information at level three or higher, followed by reading and writing for critical analysis.[10] Yet, as question one attempts to point out, how many Language Arts teachers still rely on the daily journal entry as one of the pillars of their Language Arts program?

If you answered yes to most of the questions from 1 to 14, and no to most of the questions from 15 to 23, then you could probably begin repairing four major weaknesses in your child's Language Arts program.

a)   Too many writing programs are grammatically based. The student could be writing a friendly letter to Santa or a ten page essay on the future of Castro's Cuba. Regardless, the writing in the end will be assessed based on issues surrounding grammar: spelling, sentence structure, vocabulary, usage, punctuation, paragraphs etc. True, grammar is important. But as a framework for teaching and learning writing, it is a low knowledge level skill. Ironically the same teacher will recognize 'something else' in a very good or excellent piece of writing. They will comment on an excellent cohesive essay, a wonderful idea or a unique relationship uncovered in "Bob's essay". Why? Because we all recognize a great book when we read it or a terrific movie when we see one. But what skills allowed that excellent book to become excellent? Well, it certainly wasn't only grammar! Like our imaginary writer Bob, other essayists, critics, and editors employ a host of upper level thinking skills. They analyze hundreds of attributes, call upon many perceptual skills, see dozens of relationships, detect bias, form analogies, and diverge to attain originality. Teachers appreciate the 'beauty' of those one or two pieces of excellent writing, but don't teach the upper level thinking skills urgently needed by most average students to become above average students.

b)   Too many Language Arts programs rely on completion of lengthy lists of generic writing and reading assignments. Most of these assignments require only low level thinking skills. As a result, instruction in many cases amounts to no more than a listing of topics, such as those in question four, and a posting of the due date. Placing the best samples in a portfolio doesn't make much difference either! Parents should question whether their child is really learning anything by writing a radio commercial one night and a friendly letter the next. Parents should also monitor how often these types of assignments occur year after year. There simplicity makes them easy fodder for a weak Language Arts program, and for many Language Arts teachers who neither read nor write themselves. Good teachers may assign that radio or television commercial, but prior to doing so, they will isolate and give direct instruction on analysis skills, or perceptual and creativity skills, maybe even some divergent thinking skills. In this way, thinking at a higher level becomes the goal - not bulk writing!

Parents should also take a close look a Bloom's taxonomy while they're having a closer look at their son's or daughter's reading material. The majority of questions stemming from the reading material should not be at the knowledge or comprehension level. Look for at least a 50/50 split between the upper level thinking skills and the lower level.

For without the former processes, your child may continue to hand in average to below average reports right up until the end of grade twelve.

c)   Too many Language Arts programs are simply not challenging! There are many reasons for this. The foremost reason can be found in the objectives of any single program. Is the long term goal to promote, nurture and monitor analysis, synthesis and critical thinking skills? Or is the long term goal to complete some books along with a standard set of assignments? To put it in another way - will there be many varied challenging problems to be solved, or just many pages to be filled?

What can you do as a parent? Ask what steps are being taken to define and initiate the direct teaching of an important skill such as analysis or critical thinking. Then inquire as to what novels, stories, etc. will be used as a vehicle to practice these skills. Otherwise, mastery of these important cognitive tools will only be 'hoped for' in your son or daughter.

A second frustration could be the choice of reading material. When whole language came in, text books (basal readers) went out. Choice was left up to teachers, who in the mid-80's, had money allotted to them to purchase their own class room reading materials. At that time, "I just don't know what to buy" was an often heard comment. Parents should look for a strong theme driving the choice of literature in their child's classroom. A strong theme or genre lends itself to more comparison or contrast, possible historical background and more opportunity for argumentative and opinion based essays. Good teachers can make almost any book exciting, challenging, and use it as a catalyst towards room dynamics!

d)   Parents should be aware that any end product produced by their child should be neat and tidy! Spelling should be checked and the finished product should be something the child is proud to show you.

When a student initially produces a piece of writing, there will be grammatical mistakes along with other mistakes. These should be corrected in the first draft of writing so the child does not repeatedly misspell the same words over and over again. As the child completes the second draft, more complex improvements in their writing should occur. Maybe they need to develop the plot, use more descriptive language, or go into more detail about the main character. Whatever it is, students should be constantly looking at their work with a critical eye.

Parents should be aware of this. Your child should not be bringing home a generic 'well done' or 'excellent work' if it is not a clean copy that is well thought out and reads easily.

Parents should be aware that these are objectives that need to be met when teachers teach students how to learn to write. They should be careful.....

- To ensure that students are challenged and encouraged to enjoy writing and to support students efforts to obtain a reasonable degree of success in their writing endeavors.

- To stress writing as the final proof of the application of all skills.

- To promote writing as problem solving.

- To interpret language arts with a thinking skills program.

- To increase student writing beyond the average quota within the context of two strands, a) Narrative (fiction) b) Expository.

- To study "genres", allowing for a broad historical base for both narrative and expository writing.

- To have essay topics coincide with present genre and present day world news.

- To analyze writing based on rhetorical patterns and cues.

- To create essays based on rhetorical patterns.

- To read, as well as write essays, in order to appreciate the thinking skills intrinsic to them.

- To promote higher level thinking skills.

- To implement a set of steps for writing better fiction, incorporating the analysis and synthesis of character and plot.

- To improve an individual student's vocabulary. It doesn't improve magically. It requires a lot of self discipline and teacher promotion.

- To strengthen research skills.

- To insure that editing groups are not the primary method used to analyze and correct students' work!

- To practice the introduction and the conclusion and the many skills required therein.

- To practice thinking generally and writing generally. i.e. generalizing is an upper level thinking skill.

- To practice similes, metaphors and personification. All three are good challenging mental exercises.

- To practice character study and plot, as these are only two elements which take story writing into the upper level thinking skills.

- To practice the four basic sentence patterns in the English language.

CHAPTER 9

The Dreaded Science Fair Project

Parents often dread the day their kids come home and exclaim, *"We're going to have a science fair! Could you help me with my project?"*

Well...help is at hand! Parental support and involvement is necessary. However, children need to do their own work. It is important that children work independently and display interest and initiative.

There are basically three different types of science projects; The **Experimental**, the **Innovative** and the **Research** project.

An experimental or innovative project is far stronger than a research project. However, some students are comfortable with a research project, especially if they are new to science fairs.

Many students unwittingly drift into a research type project because they are still unfamiliar with thinking processes related to science. This usually shows up in ideas expressed to the teacher or parent as:

"I want to do cars", "I want to do whales", "I want to do sports". The verb 'do' normally means go to the library and write notes and draw pictures of whales. This is not scientific thinking!

So what's missing? I believe it is the ability to wonder - wonder scientifically. It is a cognitive ability, sometimes called problem finding, and it should be taught to students. Its absence is one of the single biggest road blocks to becoming a scientific thinker instead of a taker of science notes. The best planners and forecasters use it all the time.

The following guidelines help parents to understand what is needed in each project type.

Preparing a Science Project is an opportunity for students to be involved in a real problem solving situation. It allows them to experiment with their interest, make use of their knowledge and apply skills they have learned. This experiment will help to prepare them for their future role in the real world.

As an interested parent, you can:

- Suggest project questions and ideas.

HOW WE WONDER

INCREASING LEVEL OF HYPOTHESIZING →

INCREASING MANIPULATION AND ANALYSIS OF DATA →

INCREASING AMOUNT OF HIGHER LEVEL THINKING →

Every day Wondering	Wondering in L.A./Library Research	Wondering in Math Problem Solving	Wondering in Science & Innovation
I wonder what's for lunch?	I wonder how W.W.I started?	I wonder what the % discount on the new car come to?	I wonder if tomato plants grow better in sand?
I wonder what's on T.V.?	I want to do whales.	I wonder what the perimeter of the yard is?	Will different shaped pipes drain water faster?
I wonder if my friend will call?	I want to do tanks.	I wonder how to balance the budget? the books?	Will potatoes make a better battery than lemons?
I wonder what I'll do this weekend?	I wonder how J.F.K. became President?	I wonder how to solve 15 + 5 + 5 or any other math problem level 1 to level 4	I wonder if red light or blue light will cause a solar cell to work better?
I wonder if I made the team?	I wonder what photosynthesis is?		Will my balsa glider go farther if I change the shape of the wings?

This level of wondering usually requires no answer.

△ May develop into next 3 categories.

Many View School This Way.

May involve upper level thinking and opinion, argumentation, and critical thinking.

△ May be found in other categories, from simple to complex.

- Experimentation and data collection must follow.
- **Accuracy** in measurement is also necessary.
- **Hypothesizing** is necessary.
- **Planning** is necessary to control variables.

Figure 3

- Provide transportation to libraries, businesses, museums, nature centers, universities or any such source of project information.

- Assist with technical work such as construction and photography which may be outside the child's ability or safety.

- Share the learning experience with your child.

- Set up a summer investigation of interest to your child. Wonder about something. Hypothesize and collect data daily, even if it is for five minutes a day. E.g. "I wonder if I'll catch more fish at the north or south end of the lake?"

- Purchase Lego or Fischer Technik and encourage your child to participate in design and construction. Building and designing are good for planning and problem solving.

- Have your son or daughter explain graphs found in newspapers or magazines. This is excellent for practice in interpretation and analysis.

- Take your son or daughter to work with you. Demonstrate how you have to plan, forecast, make decisions, design and collect data.

- Demonstrate, that as an adult, you hypothesize all the time. Practice it.

FORMAT OF AN EXPERIMENTAL SCIENCE PROJECT

Be careful to ensure that your child views the following science processes as ways of thinking. Many students see the science project as only a backboard with labels. Here's a tip! See the labels in their verb form. **Problem** is really problem finding or wondering. **Hypothesis** simply stems from hypothesizing. **Observation** is observing with a ruler, a stop watch and a scale etc. **Conclusion** is concluding, explaining what happened. **Application** is applying your newly found knowledge to a real world situation. These are all practical thinking skills...useful in all walks of life...whether you're bagging groceries or building skyscrapers.

Problem - This is a simple statement explaining what you are wondering about. The wondering itself is not that simple. Try starting the sentence with the word "will..."

Hypothesis - State your prediction or guess as to the outcome based on your acquired knowledge. Many students have trouble phrasing the hypothesis. To help, try the "if...then" statement outline with your son or daughter. Following "if" are usually the things your child is wondering about. These things are called independent variables. After the word "then" a student writes his guess as to what might happen. For example, your son might wonder about the many birds visiting your back yard bird feeder. A correct hypothesis might read like this: "If Blue Jays, Robins and Sparrows use the bird feeder, then Blue Jays will visit it most often".

Apparatus - Listing the equipment and materials used to perform the experiment. Your child should practice his visual imagery and see how the equipment will be set up before he starts.

Procedure - Your child should describe or explain a complete and accurate account of his procedure. Good thinkers imagine themselves going through these steps before they actually start. It only takes a few seconds and it helps to get rid of steps that may ruin the experiment. Good planners do this all the time.

Observations - This may be the most important part of the whole process. After recording all the data and anything else he's observed, he should begin looking for patterns and relationships. Students who have difficulty doing this, are often the same students who cannot see patterns or relationships in math problems or in character and plot study of novels in Language Arts. Analysis skills are vital here! Graphs are an important part of observations. This is an upper level thinking skill and requires much practice.

Conclusion - This is the part most often completed incorrectly. Most students simply repeat the results or observations here. They should be explaining **why** the results occurred. A trip to the library or the teacher may be necessary to explain a curious result!

TIPS ON PRESENTING AN EXPERIMENTAL PROJECT

1. **Type of Project**: The best projects are *experimental* in nature. A collection of information about a subject is not the best idea. The latter falls under Language Arts / library research.

2. **The Title**: It should be as simple as possible. It's a small thing, but if your son or daughter could put some imagination into it, it would help. It's like an advertisement. For example, two excellent award winning projects I remember dealt with boat keels and memory. The titles were, "You'll Keel Over", and "You're Memory - Is It Hot or Not".

FORMAT OF A RESEARCH PROJECT REPORT

The following information should be included in the final draft of the research project report:

Title page including:
- name of project
- names of participants
- date of writing
- name of school

Introduction

Discussion or Main Body of the report

Conclusions:
- Applications or Recommendations
- Acknowledgments

References

Appendix (if applicable)

FORMAT OF AN INNOVATION PROJECT REPORT

The following information should be included in the report:

Title page including:
- name of project
- names of project partners
- date of writing
- name of school

Write up your report under the following headings:
- statement of problem
- purpose of device and criteria project had to satisfy
- list of materials
- diagram with main parts labeled
- tests performed
- observations
- conclusions based on test results
- all problems anticipated
- mini problems solved

Acknowledgments

References

TIPS ON DOING AN INNOVATION PROJECT

The steps in doing this type of project are:

Have your child...Keep notes on ideas and processes she is planning to use. Make sure she understands the scientific principles behind them. She should determine the criteria she will use to evaluate the success of the prototype.

She should...Plan her device (invention). Sketches should contain parts, measurements, and how parts are connected. Detailed sketches of more complete parts can be included.

She should...Organize her material and assemble her working prototype. The first prototype need not be a final product but it should be complete enough to be functional so that it can be tested.

She should...Test the prototype to see if it lives up to expectations. The tests can be simple (does it do what it is supposed to do?) or elaborate (performing a stress test to see how much pressure or use it can withstand).

*She should...*Through her testing, determine what improvements need to be made and make improvements to the prototype until she has succeeded in making a good working model. She should pay attention to the details in the final prototype.

The success or failure of a prototype will be determined by how well it lives up to the criteria used to evaluate the success of the prototype. Her tests should be designed to evaluate the project based on these criteria. If the device is to work faster, she must test its speed. If it must withstand repeated use, she must test it for stress factors.

HOW TO MAKE THE SCIENCE DISPLAY EFFECTIVE

The Title
- The title should be brief.
- It could ask a question or be creative.

How Much Should They Write?
- Keep written material to a minimum.
- A good illustration or graphic representation can save many words.

Apparatus / Displays
- Large arrays of mechanical apparatus are unnecessary and confusing.
- It is often better to display one piece of unique equipment alongside a model, a drawing, or a photo of the complete assembly.

Graphs and Charts
- Your child should use simple bar, pie, line, or picture graphs.
- Use captions to explain graphs and charts adequately.
- Avoid scatter diagrams or line graphs that re-cross. These are too confusing for the average viewer.
- Use of colors will make the various factors more discernible.

"SORRY SIR . I CAN'T ACCEPT THIS.... SCHOOL POLICY."

PREPARING THE BACKBOARD

A backboard for the science project is usually three sided. The dimensions will vary slightly, but generally speaking its height is approximately 1.0 meters and its width side to side is approximately 1.3 meters. Some office supplies stores have ready made science backboards. The layout of a backboard should be as follows:

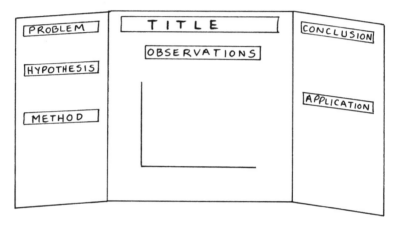

A word about competition in science fairs...or anything else.

It is my belief that anyone - whether it be a child or an adult - needs to be recognized for a job well done!

Competition has become a bad word in the school system. "We are all the same!" is the philosophy. This is not true! I believe it is dehumanizing to a child to get the same mark or recognition when he / she has mastered a concept and done exceptional work in comparison to another who has put some effort in and barely completed the job.

Intelligent people often get their incentive from a job well done and the recognition that this has happened. Mediocre work should be recognized as mediocre work. Exceptional work should be recognized as exceptional work! Otherwise children become despondent, resentful and refuse to put in their greatest effort. Why should they? Their peers down the way haven't and they got the same mark. School policies often reflect this mediocre standing. Parents need to have a voice in what happens to their children in a competitive sense.

It is my belief children don't have to feel good all the time. They need to learn to experience discouragement and failure. They need to experience the excitement of achieving excellence through study and hard work.

These are standards that our forefathers aspired to down through the ages.

Some parents want competition as an element their children can learn to deal with and aspire to. Others prefer the "feel good philosophy" for what they consider to be the psychological well being of their children. Parents should have a say in what they want for their children in regards to evaluation. Competition, marks and evaluation have been downplayed by the educational administration. Some decisions have been wise - some very foolish. Parents need to weld a partnership with educational decision makers to maintain the standards they want for their children.

CHAPTER 10

Tests Parents Should Know About

There are many reasons why parents want their children tested. Mostly they want to know if their child is up to grade level in reading, writing or math.

Some children are referred to a reading clinician. In this case, testing can cost up to $500. Others are referred to resource teachers in their local schools to be tested. Resource teachers usually use formal testing methods. Teachers also test in the regular classroom. These tests are usually designed by the teacher and test the child's mastery level in the basic curriculum.

Here are some guidelines parents can use when requesting testing be done on their children:

- Parents should state what testing they want done and why.
- They should give some background information about their child's physical and academic development.
- The family profile should be recorded. What is the family make up? Where or who does the child live with? What is the child's age, etc.
- Give the child's medical history.

A sample of formal tests available to parents are listed below. There are many more, but these are commonly used.

1. The Woodcock Johnson - Revised

   It tests for the following:
   - Memory for names
   - Memory for sentences
   - Visual matching
   - Incomplete words
   - Visual closure
   - Picture vocabulary
   - Analysis - synthesis
   - Broad Cognitive ability
   - Visual - Auditory learning

- Memory by words
- Sound blending
- Long term retrieval
- Short term memory
- Auditory processing
- Listening comprehension

2. Peabody Picture Vocabulary Test

3. Stieglitz Informal Reading Inventory

   It tests for the following:
   - Graded words in context
   - Graded words in isolation
   - Graded passages
   - This test is an indicator of where the student is performing. e.g. the independent level, the instructional level, the frustration level.

4. Bader Reading Inventory

   This tests for the child's independent reading level.

5. Barnell - Loft Diagnostic Achievement Testing Spelling

6. J.R. Gentry Developmental Spelling Test

7. Key Math - Revised - Form A

   This tests for the following:
   - Basic concepts
   - Operations
   - Applications

8. Beery Developmental Test of Visual - Math Integration

These are just a few of the formal tests available. It takes the mystery out of the testing procedures. It allows parents to put a name to some testing procedures that are available for their children. Resource teachers at your child's school can give you information about the formal tests they use. Some schools are short of funds and tests are not purchased due to the cost factor. Parents who want formal testing done should have input into what testing procedures need to be available for their children.

Classroom teachers test students on a regular basis. There are usually different kinds of tests which are designed by the teacher. Parents should make sure that these tests not only assess their child's mastery at a knowledge/comprehension level, but also in the upper thinking levels of application analysis and synthesis.

The tests your children bring home should not be just rote learning - fill in the blanks only! Good test design should reflect the curriculum being taught and the process learned. They should also include higher level thinking and problem solving.

In the following test, the children were taught "problem finding" as part of the creative problem solving, hypothesizing as part of the science process thinking, graphing, and the higher level thinking skills of interpretation, analysis and conclusions. This was all within the context of the science unit on "Population Interaction". The teacher placed the emphasis on problem finding, hypothesizing and interpreting data in the science lesson.

EXAMPLE OF A SCIENCE PROCESS TEST

PROBLEM FINDING is an important science process. It is the ability to ask questions, to wonder about things. Begin wondering about the two objects pictured below. Ask questions that can be solved through experimentation. Write three problems for each one.

1. _____
2. _____
3. _____

1. _____
2. _____
3. _____

HYPOTHESIZING is a second important science process. A hypothesis is an IF...THEN statement.

What follows the IF? _____
What follows THEN? _____

We hypothesize all the time, not just in science. Describe two examples of hypothesizing in every day life.
1. IF _____
2. IF _____

Place an S beside a science type problem.
Place an L beside a language arts research type problem.
Place an M beside a math type problem.
Place an E beside an everyday type problem.

_____ 1. Did my mom put any juice in my lunch?
_____ 2. Will grass become healthier if we cut it shorter?
_____ 3. Can I afford that new Bart Simpson T-shirt?
_____ 4. How did the Plains People live 300 years ago?
_____ 5. Do squirrels collect more acorns than berries in the fall?
_____ 6. How much paint is left if I used 2 liters but bought 8 liters?
_____ 7. Should I take my gym clothes home to be washed?
_____ 8. Will 1 cup of milk boil faster than 1 cup of water?
_____ 9. Can we grow live lobsters in an artificial environment?
_____ 10. How did WW II begin?

Assume these are problems you've wondered about. Below each problem write a HYPOTHESIS.

1. Will heat change the color of paint?

2. Do headphones harm hearing?

3. Are horses more intelligent than dogs?

4. Do people prefer Cherry 7UP or Cherry Coke?

ASSUME THE FOLLOWING HYPOTHESIS:
If garbage wrapped in X garbage bags, Y garbage bags and Z garbage bags is pushed down a flight of stairs, then the Y garbage bags will contain their garbage best.

List 5 variables you would control while running this experiment.
1. _____
2. _____

3. _____
4. _____
5. _____

Describe 2 variables you controlled in your own experiment.
1. _____
2. _____

What story is each of these graphs telling?

ENGINE TEMPERATURE

HOURS

ORANGES EATEN

VITAMIN C

TEST MARKS   100%

HOURS STUDYING

HOUSE PRICES $

J F M A M J J A S O N D
MONTHS

Describe the relationship(s) you see in the following data.

Maximum distance reached in a 26 KM race by:

Smokers	Non Smokers	Vegetarian Smokers
18km	20km	19km
15km	21km	21km
15km	22km	21km
17km	26km	19km
16km	26km	20km
14km	21km	19km
15km	23km	23km

Your conclusion: _____
_____
_____

Assume these are your observations of 6 bears over six years. Your hypothesis was: IF the same bears experience cold autumns and warm autumns, THEN these bears will hibernate later in a warm autumn.

Bears	1990 warm	1991 cold	1992 cold	1993 cold	1994 cold	1995 warm
Bob	O	D	D	D	D	O
Reg	O	D	D	N	D	O
Bif	O	N	D	D	D	O
Sue	O	D	D	D	D	O
Big Guy	N	N	N	N	N	N
Jon	O	D	D	D	N	O

O = October   N = November   D = December

Your conclusion: _____

_____

_____

Now design your own graph using the data on bears.

CHAPTER 11

The Parent / Teacher Interview

Parents need to be prepared for the parent / teacher interview. Usually they are quite short in length - 15 to 20 minutes. Be ready with questions! Add any information you think is beneficial for the teacher to know. If you need more time with the teacher, pre-plan so you can meet when more time is available. There is no law that states you have to meet the teacher on the prescribed interview night. It is quite reasonable to request another time after school when you don't feel the pressure of time constraints. Keep that in mind.

There are some basic steps that should be taken to prepare yourself for the interview.

1. Make sure you get samples of your child's work **prior** to the interview time. If the teacher is not accustomed to sending work samples home, contact the teacher and request it. Take a close look at the work. Write down observations and questions as you look through it.
2. If there is a problem you want to discuss with the teacher, make sure you state the situation in a non confrontational manner. There is nothing as emotional as dealing with problems concerning your child. Most teachers want to work with parents and are genuinely concerned about the child's well being. Parents should not be afraid to confront a problem area with the teacher - communication between parent and teacher is essential for improvements and changes to occur. However, teachers too have their breaking point. When a parent talks to a teacher in a confrontational manner, it is human nature to be defensive.
3. If the parent feels the teacher is not listening or their problem is not resolved, it is prudent to meet with the principal and the teacher to resolve the problem. Sometimes a third party is useful for mediation purposes.
4. There are some questions parents should be asking:
   - How is my child functioning in Math, Language Arts, Science, etc.?

- How is my child relating and interacting with the other children?
- Is my child at grade level? Above or below grade level? How do you know?
- Tell me some strengths you see in my child.
- Is my child participating in some enrichment activities? What are they?
- What tests and reporting methods do you use?

Suggestions made to the teacher are beneficial if your child is having discipline problems or problems with academic progress.

Suggest a contract be drawn up between home and school where the child must meet certain behaviors. For example, if the child picks fights at school, or is rude to the teacher, or is constantly late for school, or doesn't get homework done, consequences have to be spelled out! This contract should outline the expected responsibilities of the child and the consequences given out to the child by the home and the school.

Set up a time on a weekly basis where you and the teacher can communicate with each other and monitor the child's progress. Contracts are helpful because bad habits are learned. Constant remedies and reinforcements can change these learned behaviors.

Remember! The parent / teacher interview times are set aside for parents and teachers to share information about your child's academic and personal development.

These interview times are useful in that they provide you with the opportunity to establish communication with your child's teacher.

There, you and the teacher can mutually decide on any future plans or strategies that can be beneficial for your child.

CHAPTER 12

NOTES

Parents are an important part of the educational society. To reiterate, the more parents know about the system and its educational practices, the better it is for the children! Parents need to be able to step inside the system, and ask questions about the fads and trends that readily occur. Being aware of the fetish for innovative ideas that most educators have, should make parents vigilant about asking if this new innovation will promote better educational practices for their children, and provide school environments that center on the well being of the child.

"Out with the old," and "In with the new," leaves parents in a quandary about what is good or what is once more recycled as a new idea. Substantial reasons should be given to parents whenever their children are made part of a new reform. Mindless experimentation and a good sales pitch is not adequate. Educators have been too hasty in passing off traditional teaching techniques as "old news", and eagerly embracing every new fad that comes along. Parents need to be the watch dogs of such blatant whims.

Recently, schools have taken on the burden of becoming "all things to all people". Well and good to have family life programs, drug education, multicultural pursuits and environmental awareness projects - but how much can be effectively accomplished when the teacher's time, and the student's focus is spread too thinly? If parents want their children to become better writers, competent mathematicians and scientific thinkers, more time has to be spent on these basic concepts!

Part of the problem lies in that there is little (if any) consistency in programs or standards from school to school in the public school system. This is confusing to any family moving several blocks down the road! Consequently, many are retreating to the private school setting to regain some semblance of conforming curriculum and evaluation standards.

A disproportionate amount of time and resources is given to the control and rehabilitation of disruptive students in public schools. Parents are now demanding a voice in the goal setting and evaluation of programs placed in their children's school. This includes input into disruptive behavior concerns, as well as other particular programs. They are not so ready to embrace every new idea that comes along. Reflection is becoming part of the public system. They want less attention to "frills" and more emphasis placed on the basic skills and thinking strategy programs.

All of this has resulted in the alarms being sent out over educational funding cut backs. Parents are asking, "Where has all the money gone?" The growth of bureaucracy in the modern school system has grown to epidemic proportions! Like any disease it weakens the body. Top heavy administration, and every new fad coming along has fed this bureaucracy. Now the pot is empty. Parents have to take serious consideration to what monies are leaving the public purse to ensure every cent is spent judiciously. Specific, not general questions, need to be asked about who is paid what..., how much... and why. They need to question if the money is spent efficiently and proportionately. When educators and administrators attend conferences, the public funding for these conferences should be justified by the resulting impact on the direct education of the children in the classroom. When new initiatives are introduced, the price of the venture should be included as parents are being persuaded to welcome it in their schools. Educational funding cutbacks place new responsibilities on parents to ensure their children are not "short changed".

Never before has the opportunity been so right for educators to bond with parents and form a partnership that will allow the school system in North America to once again become one of the best in the world! Quality people have to be placed in strategic positions to ensure that the children receive the best possible education. Dedicated teachers, willing to put the extra effort in, are essential. Teachers themselves must be highly motivated in order to motivate their students. Teachers want to be regarded as professionals but often feel they are not a part of the day to day decision making. The Economic Council of Canada (1992) states that teachers who dislike teaching often strive for administrative positions.[11] We need a different quality administrator. One who works with the children on a daily basis, teaches, and promotes team work amongst the staff. In addition, academic leaders should be academics. Too often schools are run by politically motivated people who are more interested in having the power and being the so called boss. An effective administrator is one who has a good understanding of pedagogical practices and interacts with students on a regular basis. Everyone knows our hope is in educating our youth. This is one time we don't want to get a failing grade!

BIBLIOGRAPHY

1 Leith and Smith, "The Three Component Approach to Teaching," (University of Manitoba, 1982)

2 Barry K. Beyer, "Developing a Thinking Skills Program," (Boston: Allyn and Bacon Inc., 1988) p.2.

3 Ibid; p.35.

4 Arthur Whimbey and Jack Lockhead, "Problem Solving and Comprehension," (Philadelphia: Franklin Institute Press, 1982)

5 Ibid; p.18.

6 Dr. Willard R. Daggett, "Preparing For Employment in the 21st Century: The Challenge to Education," (Waterloo: National Institute, 1991)

7 Arthur Whimbey and Jack Lockhead, "Problem Solving and Comprehension," (Philadelphia: Franklin Institute Press, 1982)

8 Barry K. Beyer, "Developing a Thinking Skills Program," (Boston: Allyn and Bacon Inc, 1988) p.61.

9 Dr. Deborah E. Burns, "Methods and Materials for the Direct Teaching of Thinking Skills", (University of Connecticut: 1990)

10 Dr. Willard R. Daggett, "Preparing For Employment in the 21st Century: The Challenge to Education", (Waterloo: National Institute, 1991)

11 The Economic Council of Canada, "A Lot to Learn: Education and Training in Canada", (Ottawa: Canada Communication Group Publishing, 1992), p.12.

ABOUT THE AUTHOR

Joy Smith has been an educator for 18 years. During that time, she was a classroom teacher and a consultant for gifted education. She achieved her Masters Degree in curriculum design with a major in Math and Science.

She won the Hedley Award for her development of the "Three Component Approach to Teaching" in her Masters year.

Joy has contributed greatly to the publication of various Science textbooks.

She has lectured in Canada, the United States and England.

Recently, she has become a strong advocate for the necessity of parental involvement in education.

Her vested interest in education is inspired by her six children.

GIVE "LIES MY KID'S TEACHER TOLD ME" TO A FRIEND!

EDUCATIONAL ENTERPRISES
Box 2063
Winnipeg, Manitoba   R3C 3R4
CANADA

Send to:

Name: _____

Address: _____

City: _____

Province/State _____ Postal Code/Zip Code _____

Please send me_____copies
Enclosed is $9.95 (Cdn funds) per book (includes tax, postage and handling).

Amount enclosed $_____
Make cheque or money order payable to
"Educational Enterprises"

- -

GIVE "LIES MY KID'S TEACHER TOLD ME" TO A FRIEND!

EDUCATIONAL ENTERPRISES
Box 2063
Winnipeg, Manitoba   R3C 3R4
CANADA

Send to:

Name: _____

Address: _____

City: _____

Province/State _____ Postal Code/Zip Code _____

Please send me_____copies
Enclosed is $9.95 (Cdn funds) per book (includes tax, postage and handling).

Amount enclosed $_____
Make cheque or money order payable to
"Educational Enterprises"